WORKS AND LIVES

The Anthropologist as Author

The Harry Camp Lectures at Stanford University

The Harry Camp Memorial Fund was established in
1959 to make possible a continuing series of lectures
at Stanford University on topics bearing on the dignity
and worth of the human individual.

WORKS AND LIVES

The Anthropologist as Author

CLIFFORD GEERTZ

Stanford University Press   *1988*
Stanford, California

Stanford University Press, Stanford, California
© 1988 by the Board of Trustees of the Leland Stanford Junior University
Printed in the United States of America

Library of Congress Cataloging-in-Publication Data

Geertz, Clifford.
  Works and lives: the anthropologist as author / Clifford Geertz.
    p.   cm.
  Includes index.
  ISBN 0-8047-1428-2 (alk. paper)
    I. Ethnology—Authorship.   I. Title.
GN307.7.G44   1988   87-20310
306—dc19   CIP

PREFACE

The first four chapters of this volume were given, in somewhat different form, as the Harry Camp Memorial Lectures at Stanford University in the Spring of 1983; the third chapter has also been previously published in *Raritan*, Fall 1983.

A few preliminary caveats are necessary, not in the way of apology, which won't help, but for the sake of clarity. First, the term "anthropology" is used here mainly as equivalent to "ethnography" or "works based on ethnography." This usage, though common to the point of being standard, is, of course, inexact. I am quite aware that archaeology, comparative linguistics, physical anthropology, and various other forms of study not, or not necessarily, ethnographically based exist and have as valid a claim to be included in the "anthropology" rubric as does "ethnography" and that they raise discourse issues special to themselves. I use the term to refer to sociocultural anthropology, and particularly to that part of it that is ethnographically oriented, merely for the sake of expository convenience. This use carries no suggestion that the sort of work I discuss exhausts the referent of the term or that such work is more deserving of it than other sorts.

The second caveat is that although both biographical and historical matters inevitably enter my discussion at numerous points, this study is not itself either biographical or historical in intent, but is primarily concerned with "how anthropologists write"—that is, it is textually oriented. I am emphatically not one of those who believe in wholly autonomous "ontological" texts, and doubtless biographical and historical matters are far from irrelevant to the interpretation of anthropological works. My stress here, however, is on other, if you will "literary," matters, normally much less attended to in discussions of anthropology.

A large number of people have commented on one or another aspect of the manuscript, pro, con, and otherwise, and if I single out Professors Karen Blu and Amelie Rorty for explicit mention and particular (and particularly heartfelt) thanks, it is only because their efforts were extensive and have had a substantial effect on the final form of what appears here. I am grateful to everyone who has taken the time to try to help me find my way out of my own particular flybottle.

Finally, in lieu of a dedication, which would be presumptuous, I would like merely to mention the name of the man, nowhere cited in the body of the text, who has had no direct connection to it or me, but whose work has served as its governing inspiration at almost every point: Kenneth Burke.

The Institute for Advanced Study   C.G.
Princeton, N.J.
February 1987

CONTENTS

WORKS AND LIVES

The Anthropologist as Author

BEING THERE

Anthropology and the Scene of Writing

The illusion that ethnography is a matter of sorting strange and irregular facts into familiar and orderly categories—this is magic, that is technology—has long since been exploded. What it is instead, however, is less clear. That it might be a kind of writing, putting things to paper, has now and then occurred to those engaged in producing it, consuming it, or both. But the examination of it as such has been impeded by several considerations, none of them very reasonable.

One of these, especially weighty among the producers, has been simply that it is an unanthropological sort of thing to do. What a proper ethnographer ought properly to be doing is going out to places, coming back with information about how people live there, and making that information available to the professional community in practical form, not lounging about in libraries reflecting on literary questions. Excessive concern, which in practice usually means any concern at all, with how ethnographic texts are constructed seems like an unhealthy self-absorption—time-wasting at best, hypochondriacal at worst. What we want to know about is the Tikopians and the Tallensi, not the narrative strategies of Raymond Firth or the rhetorical machinery of Meyer Fortes.

Another objection, here coming mostly from the consumer side, is that anthropological texts are not worth such delicate attention. It is one thing to investigate how a Conrad, a Flaubert, or even a Balzac, gets his effects; to engage in such an enterprise for a Lowie or a Radcliffe-Brown, to speak only of the dead, seems comic. A few anthropologists—Sapir, Benedict, Malinowski, and these days Lévi-Strauss—may be recognized as having a distinctive literary style, and not being above an occasional trope. But that is unusual and somewhat to their disadvantage—suggestive even of sharp practice. Good anthropological texts are plain texts, unpretending. They neither invite literary-critical close reading nor reward it.

But perhaps the most intense objection, coming from all quarters, and indeed rather general to intellectual life these days, is that concentrating our gaze on the ways in which knowledge claims are advanced undermines our capacity to take any of those claims seriously. Somehow, attention to such matters as imagery, metaphor, phraseology, or voice is supposed to lead to a corrosive relativism in which everything is but a more or less clever expression of opinion. Ethnography becomes, it is said, a mere game of words, as poems and novels are supposed to be. Exposing how the thing is done is to suggest that, like the lady sawed in half, it isn't done at all.

These views are unreasonable, because they are not based on the experience of threats present and actual, or even looming, but on the imagining of possible ones that might occur were everything to be suddenly otherwise than it now is. If anthropologists were to stop reporting how

2

things are done in Africa and Polynesia, if they were instead to spend their time trying to find double plots in Alfred Kroeber or unreliable narrators in Max Gluckman, and if they were seriously to argue that Edward Westermarck's stories about Morocco and those of Paul Bowles relate to their subject in the same way, with the same means and the same purposes, matters would indeed be in a parlous state.

But that all this would be brought on if anthropological writing were taken seriously as writing is hard to credit. The roots of fear must lie elsewhere: in the sense, perhaps, that should the literary character of anthropology be better understood, some professional myths about how it manages to persuade would be impossible to maintain. In particular, it might be difficult to defend the view that ethnographic texts convince, insofar as they do convince, through the sheer power of their factual substantiality. The marshaling of a very large number of highly specific cultural details has been the major way in which the look of truth—verisimilitude, *vraisemblance, Wahrscheinlichkeit*—has been sought in such texts. Whatever doubts the oddness of the material induces in the reader are to be overcome by its sheer abundance. Yet the fact is that the degree of credence, whether high, low, or otherwise, actually given to Malinowski's, Lévi-Strauss's, or anybody else's ethnography does not rest, at least not primarily, on such a basis. If it did, J. G. Frazer, or anyway Oscar Lewis, would indeed be king, and the suspension of disbelief many people (myself included) accord to Edmund Leach's data-poor *Political Systems of Highland Burma*, or Margaret Mead's impressionistic essay, *Balinese Character*, would be inexplicable. Ethnographers may indeed think they are believed for the extensiveness of their descriptions. (Leach attempted to answer the empiricist attacks on his Burma book by writing a fact-crammed one on

3

Sri Lanka, but it has been far less attended to. Mead argued that Gregory Bateson's hundreds of photographs demonstrated her arguments, but hardly anyone, including Bateson, much agreed with her.) Perhaps ethnographers should be believed for the extensiveness of their descriptions, but that does not seem to be the way it works.

Just why the idea persists that it does so work is difficult to say. Perhaps old-fashioned notions about how "findings" are "established" in the harder sciences has something to do with it. In any case, the main alternative to this sort of factualist theory of how anthropological works convince, namely that they do so through the force of their theoretical arguments, is no more plausible. Malinowski's theoretical apparatus, once a proud tower indeed, lies largely in ruins, but he remains the ethnographer's ethnographer. The rather passé quality that Mead's psychological, culture-and-personality speculations now seem to have (*Balinese Character* was supported by a grant for the study of dementia praecox, which the Balinese were supposed to display in a walking-around form) doesn't seem to detract very much from the cogency of her observations, unmatched by any of the rest of us, concerning what the Balinese are like. Some, at least, of Lévi-Strauss's work will survive the dissolution of structuralism into its all-too-eager successors. People will read *The Nuer* even if, as it has tended to, segmentary theory hardens into a dogma.

The ability of anthropologists to get us to take what they say seriously has less to do with either a factual look or an air of conceptual elegance than it has with their capacity to convince us that what they say is a result of their having actually penetrated (or, if you prefer, been penetrated by) another form of life, of having, one way or another, truly

4

"been there." And that, persuading us that this offstage miracle has occurred, is where the writing comes in.

《》

The crucial peculiarities of ethnographic writing are, like the purloined letter, so fully in view as to escape notice: the fact, for example, that so much of it consists in incorrigible assertion. The highly situated nature of ethnographic description—this ethnographer, in this time, in this place, with these informants, these commitments, and these experiences, a representative of a particular culture, a member of a certain class—gives to the bulk of what is said a rather take-it-or-leave-it quality. "Vas you dere, Sharlie?" as Jack Pearl's Baron Munchausen used to say.

Even if, as is now increasingly the case, others are working in the same area or on the same group, so that at least some general checking is possible, it is very difficult to disprove what someone not transparently uninformed has said. One can go look at Azande again, but if the complex theory of passion, knowledge, and causation that Evans-Pritchard said he discovered there isn't found, we are more likely to doubt our own powers than we are to doubt his— or perhaps simply to conclude that the Zande are no longer themselves. Whatever the state of thinking about the nature of *kula* exchange may or may not be at the moment, and it is rapidly changing, the picture of it given in *Argonauts of the Western Pacific* remains for all practical purposes ineffaceable. Those who would like to lessen its force must contrive somehow to shift our attention to other pictures. Even in the case of what in most other sorts of empirical study would be taken to be direct contradiction (Robert Redfield and Oscar Lewis on Tepotzlan, for example), the tendency, when both scholars are reputable, is to regard the problem as stemming from different sorts of minds taking hold of different parts of the elephant—a third opinion would but add to the embarrassment. It is not that everything ethnographers say is accepted once and for all simply because they say it. A very great deal, thank God, is not. It is that the grounds upon which it is or it isn't accepted are extremely person-specific. Unable to recover the immediacies of field work for empirical reinspection, we listen to some voices and ignore others.

This would be rather a scandal if we listened to some and not to others—the matter is relative, of course—out of whim, habit, or (a favored account nowadays) prejudice or political desire. But if we do so because some ethnographers are more effective than others in conveying in their prose the impression that they have had close-in contact with far-out lives, the matter may be less desperate. In discovering how, in this monograph or that article, such an impression is created, we shall discover, at the same time, the criteria by which to judge them. As the criticism of fiction and poetry grows best out of an imaginative engagement with fiction and poetry themselves, not out of imported notions about what they should be, the criticism of anthropological writing (which is in a strict sense neither, and in a broad one both) ought to grow out of a similar engagement with *it*, not out of preconceptions of what it must look like to qualify as a science.

Given the person-specific (*not* "personal") nature of our judgments in these matters, the obvious place to begin such an engagement is with the question of what, in anthropology, an "author" is. It may be that in other realms of discourse the author (along with man, history, the self, God, and other middle-class appurtenances) is in the process of dying; but he . . . she . . . is still very much alive among an-

6

thropologists. In our ingenuous discipline, perhaps as usual an episteme behind, it still very much matters who speaks.

I make these irreverent allusions to Michel Foucault's famous article, "What Is an Author?" (which in fact I agree with, save for its premises, its conclusions, and its cast of mind), because, whatever one thinks of a world in which all forms of discourse would be reduced to "the anonymity of a murmur" in the interests of the dispersion of power, or of the notion that Mallarmé marks a decisive rupture in the history of literature, after which the notion of a literary work is steadily displaced by one of textual modes of domination, it does locate the question I am posing with some exactness. Foucault distinguishes there, perhaps a bit too sharply, between two realms of discourse: those, most especially fiction (though history, biography, philosophy, and poetry as well), in which what he calls the "author-function" remains, for the moment anyway, reasonably strong; and those, especially science (but also private letters, legal contracts, political broadsides), in which, for the most part, it does not. This is not a constant matter, even within our own tradition: in the Middle Ages, most tales—the *Chanson de Roland*—had no authors; most scientific treatises—the *Almagest*—had them. But

a reversal occurred in the seventeenth or eighteenth century. Scientific discourses began to be received for themselves, in the anonymity of an established or always redemonstrable truth; their membership in a systematic ensemble, and not the reference to the individual who produced them, stood as their guarantee. The author-function faded away, and the inventor's name served only to christen a theorem, a proposition, particular effect, property, body, group of elements, or pathological syndrome. By the same token, literary discourses came to be accepted only when endowed with the author-function. We now ask of each poetic or fictional text: from where does it come, who wrote it, when, under what

7

circumstances, or beginning with what design? The meaning ascribed to it and the status or value accorded it depend upon the manner in which we answer these questions. . . . As a result, the author-function today plays an important [though, again, in Foucault's view, decreasing] role in our view of literary works.[1]

It is clear that, in these terms, anthropology is pretty much entirely on the side of "literary" discourses rather than "scientific" ones. Personal names are attached to books and articles, more occasionally to systems of thought ("Radcliffe-Brownian Functionalism"; "Lévi-Straussian Structuralism"). They are not, with very few exceptions, connected to findings, properties, or propositions ("a Murdock Marriage" is a polemical joke; "the Westermarck Effect"— its reality aside—might just qualify). This does not make us into novelists any more than constructing hypotheses or writing formulas makes us, as some seem to think, into physicists. But it does suggest some family resemblances that we tend, like the North African mule who talks always of his mother's brother, the horse, but never of his father, the donkey, to suppress in favor of others, supposedly more reputable.

《》

If, then, we admit that ethnographies tend to look at least as much like romances as they do like lab reports (though, as with our mule, not really like either), two questions, or perhaps the same one doubly asked, immediately pose themselves: (1) How is the "author-function" (or shall we, so long as we are going to be literary about the matter, just say "the author"?) made manifest in the text? (2) Just what is it—beyond the obvious tautology, "a work"—that

[1]M. Foucault, "What Is an Author?" in J. V. Harari, ed., *Textual Strategies* (Ithaca, N.Y., 1979), pp. 149–50.

the author authors? The first question, call it that of signature, is a matter of the construction of a writerly identity. The second, call it that of discourse, is a matter of developing a way of putting things—a vocabulary, a rhetoric, a pattern of argument—that is connected to that identity in such a way that it seems to come from it as a remark from a mind.

The question of signature, the establishment of an authorial presence within a text, has haunted ethnography from very early on, though for the most part it has done so in a disguised form. Disguised, because it has been generally cast not as a narratological issue, a matter of how best to get an honest story honestly told, but as an epistemological one, a matter of how to prevent subjective views from coloring objective facts. The clash between the expository conventions of author-saturated texts and those of author-evacuated ones that grows out of the particular nature of the ethnographic enterprise is imagined to be a clash between seeing things as one would have them and seeing them as they really are.

A number of unfortunate results have arisen from this burial of the question of how ethnographical texts are "author-ized" beneath anxieties (to my mind, rather exaggerated anxieties) about subjectivity. Among them is an empiricism extreme even for the social sciences; but one of the more mischievous has been that although the ambiguities implicit in that question have been deeply and continuously felt, it has been extremely difficult to address them directly. Anthropologists are possessed of the idea that the central methodological issues involved in ethnographic description have to do with the mechanics of knowledge—the legitimacy of "empathy," "insight," and the like as forms of cognition; the verifiability of internalist accounts of other peoples' thoughts and feelings; the ontological status of culture. Accordingly, they have traced their difficulties in constructing such descriptions to the problematics of field work rather than to those of discourse. If the relation between observer and observed (rapport) can be managed, the relation between author and text (signature) will follow—it is thought—of itself.

It is not merely that this is untrue, that no matter how delicate a matter facing the other might be it is not the same sort of thing as facing the page. The difficulty is that the oddity of constructing texts ostensibly scientific out of experiences broadly biographical, which is after all what ethnographers do, is thoroughly obscured. The signature issue, as the ethnographer confronts it, or as it confronts the ethnographer, demands both the Olympianism of the unauthorial physicist and the sovereign consciousness of the hyperauthorial novelist, while not in fact permitting either. The first brings charges of insensitivity, of treating people as objects, of hearing the words but not the music, and, of course, of ethnocentrism. The second brings charges of impressionism, of treating people as puppets, of hearing music that doesn't exist, and, of course, of ethnocentrism. Small wonder that most ethnographers tend to oscillate uncertainly between the two, sometimes in different books, more often in the same one. Finding somewhere to stand in a text that is supposed to be at one and the same time an intimate view and a cool assessment is almost as much of a challenge as gaining the view and making the assessment in the first place.

A sense for this challenge—how to sound like a pilgrim and a cartographer at the same time—and for the uneasiness it produces, as well as for the degree to which it is repre-

sented as arising from the complexities of self/other nego-
tiations rather than those of self/text ones, is of course only
to be gained from looking at ethnographies themselves.
And, since the challenge and the uneasiness are obviously
felt from the jacket flap on, a good place to look in looking
at ethnographies is at beginnings—at the scene-setting,
task-describing, self-presenting opening pages. So let me
take, then, to indicate more clearly what I am talking about,
two examples, one from a classic ethnography deservedly regarded as a model study, calm and magisterial, and one from
a quite recent one, also very well done, that breathes the air
of the nervous present.

The classic work is Raymond Firth's *We, the Tikopia*,
first published in 1936. After two introductions, one by Malinowski, which says Firth's book "strengthens our conviction
that cultural anthropology need not be a jumble of slogans
or labels, a factory of impressionistic short-cuts, or guess-
work reconstructions [but rather] a social science—I almost
feel tempted to say, the science among social studies," and
one by Firth, which stresses the necessity of "lengthy personal contact with the people [one studies]" and apologizes
for the fact that "this account represents not the field-work
of yesterday but that of seven years ago," the book itself begins its first chapter, "In Primitive Polynesia":

In the cool of the early morning, just before sunrise, the bow of
the *Southern Cross* headed towards the eastern horizon, on which
a tiny dark blue outline was faintly visible. Slowly it grew into a
rugged mountain mass, standing up sheer from the ocean; then as
we approached within a few miles it revealed around its base a narrow ring of low, flat land, thick with vegetation. The sullen grey
day with its lowering clouds strengthened my grim impression of
a solitary peak, wild and stormy, upthrust in a waste of waters.
  In an hour or so we were close inshore and could see canoes

11

coming round from the south, outside the reef, on which the tide was low. The outrigger-fitted craft drew near, the men in them bare to the waist, girdled with bark-cloth, large fans stuck in the backs of their belts, tortoise-shell rings or rolls of leaf in the ear-lobes and nose, bearded, and with long hair flowing loosely over their shoulders. Some plied the rough heavy paddles, some had finely plaited pandanus-leaf mats resting on the thwarts beside them, some had large clubs or spears in their hands. The ship anchored on a short cable in the open bay off the coral reef. Almost before the chain was down the natives began to scramble aboard, coming over the side by any means that offered, shouting fiercely to each other and to us in a tongue of which not a word was understood by the Mota-speaking folk of the mission vessel. I wondered how such turbulent human material could ever be induced to submit to scientific study.

Vahihaloa, my "boy," looked over the side from the upper deck, "My word, me fright too much," he said with a quavering laugh; "me tink this fella man he savvy kaikai me." *Kaikai* is the pidgin-English term for "eat." For the first time, perhaps, he began to doubt the wisdom of having left what was to him the civilization of Tulagi, the seat of Government four hundred miles away, in order to stay with me for a year in this far-off spot among such wild-looking savages. Feeling none too certain myself of the reception that awaited us—though I knew that it would stop short of cannibalism—I reassured him, and we began to get out the stores. Later we went ashore in one of the canoes. As we came to the edge of the reef our craft halted on account of the falling tide. We slipped overboard on to the coral rock and began to wade ashore hand in hand with our hosts, like children at a party, exchanging smiles in lieu of anything more intelligible or tangible at the moment. We were surrounded by crowds of naked chattering youngsters, with their pleasant light-brown velvet skins and straight hair, so different from the Melanesians we had left behind. They darted about splashing like a shoal of fish, some of them falling bodily into pools in their enthusiasm. At last the long wade ended, we climbed up the steeply shelving beach, crossed the soft, dry sand strewn with the brown needles of the Casuarina trees—a home-like touch; it was like a pine avenue—and were led to an old chief, clad with great dignity in a white coat and a loin-cloth, who awaited us on his stool under a large shady tree.[2]

There can be little doubt from this that Firth was, in every sense of the word, "there." All the fine detail, marshaled with Dickensian exuberance and Conradian fatality—the blue mass, lowering clouds, excited jabberings, velvet skins, shelved beach, needle carpet, enstooled chief—conduce to a conviction that what follows, five hundred pages of resolutely objectified description of social customs—the Tikopia do this, the Tikopia believe that—can be taken as fact. Firth's anxieties about inducing "such turbulent human material . . . to admit to scientific study" turned out to be as overdrawn as those of his "boy" that he would be eaten.

But they also never quite disappeared. The "this happened to me" accents reappear periodically; the text is nervously signed and re-signed throughout. To its last line, Firth struggles with his relation to what he has written, still seeing it in field-method terms. "The greatest need," that last line goes, "in the social sciences to-day is for a more refined methodology, as objective and dispassionate as possible, in which, while the assumptions due to the conditioning and personal interest of the investigator must influence his findings, that bias shall be consciously faced, the possibility of other initial assumptions be realized and allowance be made for the implications of each in the course of the analysis" (p. 488). At deeper levels his anxieties and those of his "boy" may not in fact have been so entirely different. "I give this somewhat egoistic recital," he writes apologetically after reviewing his field techniques, his language abilities, his mode of life on the island, and so forth, "not because I think that

[2]R. Firth, *We, the Tikopia* (London, 1936), pp. 1–2. For a contextualization of this passage in "travel writing," see now M. L. Pratt, "Fieldwork in Common Places," in J. Clifford and G. E. Marcus, eds., *Writing Culture: The Poetics and Politics of Ethnography* (Berkeley, Calif., 1986), pp. 35–37.

anthropology should be made light reading . . . but because some account of the relations of the anthropologist to his people is relevant to the nature of his results. It is an index to their social digestion—some folk cannot stomach an outsider, others absorb him easily" (p. 11).

The recent text whose opening pages I want to instance as displaying the authorial uneasiness that arises from having to produce scientific texts from biographical experiences is *The Death Rituals of Rural Greece*, by a young ethnographer, Loring Danforth. Like many of his generation, weaned on *Positivismuskritik* and anti-colonialism, Danforth seems more concerned that he will swallow his subjects than that they will swallow him, but the problem is still seen to be essentially epistemological. I quote, with a good deal of ellipsis, from his introduction, called "Self and Other":

Anthropology inevitably involves an encounter with the Other. All too often, however, the ethnographic distance that separates the reader of anthropological texts and the anthropologist himself from the Other is rigidly maintained and at times even artificially exaggerated. In many cases this distancing leads to an exclusive focus on the Other as primitive, bizarre, and exotic. The gap between a familiar "we" and an exotic "they" is a major obstacle to a meaningful understanding of the Other, an obstacle that can only be overcome through some form of participation in the world of the Other.

The maintenance of this ethnographic distance has resulted in . . . the parochialization or the folklorization of the anthropological inquiry into death. Rather than confronting the universal significance of death, anthropologists have often trivialized death by concerning themselves with the exotic, curious, and at times violent ritual practices that accompany death in many societies. . . . If, however, it is possible to reduce the distance between the anthropologist and the Other, to bridge the gap between "us" and "them," then the goal of a truly humanistic anthropology can be achieved. . . . [This] desire to collapse the distance between Self and Other which prompted [my] adoption of this [approach] springs from my fieldwork. Whenever I observed death rituals in rural Greece, I was acutely aware of a paradoxical sense of simultaneous distance and closeness, otherness and oneness. . . . To my eyes funeral laments, black mourning dress, and exhumation rites *were* exotic. Yet . . . I was conscious at all times that it is not just Others who die. I was aware that my friends and relatives will die, that I will die, that death comes to all, Self and Other alike.

Over the course of my fieldwork these "exotic" rites became meaningful, even attractive alternatives to the experience of death as I had known it. As I sat by the body of a man who had died several hours earlier and listened to his wife, his sisters, and his daughters lament his death, I imagined these rites being performed and these laments being sung at the death of my relatives, at my own death. . . . When the brother of the deceased entered the room, the women . . . began to sing a lament about two brothers who were violently separated as they sat clinging to each other in the branches of a tree that was being swept away by a raging torrent. I thought of my own brother and cried. The distance between Self and Other had grown small indeed.[3]

There are of course great differences in these two scene-settings and self-locatings: one a realistic novel model (Trollope in the South Seas), the other a philosophical meditation model (Heidegger in Greece); one a scientistic worry about being insufficiently detached, the other a humanistic worry about being insufficiently engaged. Rhetorical expansiveness in 1936, rhetorical earnestness in 1982. But there are even greater similarities, all of them deriving from a com-

[3]L. Danforth, *The Death Rituals of Rural Greece* (Princeton, N.J., 1982), pp. 5–7. For a similar modern or post-modern complaint about "the anthropology of death," growing out of a personal experience, the accidental death of his wife, in the field, see R. Rosaldo, "Grief and a Headhunter's Rage: On the Cultural Force of Emotions," in E. Bruner, ed., *Text, Play, and Story, 1983 Proceedings of the American Ethnological Society* (Washington, D.C., 1984), pp. 178–95. "[In] most anthropological studies of death, analysts simply eliminate the emotions by assuming the position of the most detached observer. Their stance also equates the ritual with the obligatory, ignores the relation between ritual and everyday life, and conflates the ritual process with the process of mourning. The general rule . . . seems to be that one should tidy things up as much as possible by wiping away the tears and ignoring the tantrums" (p. 189).

mon *topos*—the delicate but successful establishment of a familiar sensibility, much like our own, in an intriguing but unfamiliar place, not at all like our own. Firth's coming-into-the-country drama ends with his encounter, a royal audience almost, with the chief. After that, one knows they will come to understand one another, all will be well. Danforth's haunted reflections on Otherness end with his echoic mourning, more fantasy than empathy. After that, one knows the gap will be bridged, communion is at hand. Ethnographers need to convince us (as these two quite effectively do) not merely that they themselves have truly "been there," but (as they also do, if rather less obviously) that had we been there we should have seen what they saw, felt what they felt, concluded what they concluded.

Not all ethnographies, not most even, begin by grasping the horns of the signature dilemma in so emphatic a manner as do these. Most attempt rather to keep it at bay, either by starting off with extended and often enough (given what follows) overly detailed descriptions of the natural environment, population, and the like, or by extended theoretical discussions not again very much referred to. Explicit representations of authorial presence tend to be relegated, like other embarrassments, to prefaces, notes, or appendixes.

But the issue always appears, however resisted, however disguised. "The traveller in West Africa," Meyer Fortes writes on the first page of his Tallensi study (perhaps the most thoroughly objectivized of the great ethnographies—it reads like a law text written by a botanist) "who enters this region from the south is impressed by the contrast with the forest belt. According to his predilections he will view it with pleasure or dismay after the massive and gigantic gloom of the forest."[4] There is no doubt who that "traveller"

[4]M. Fortes, *The Dynamics of Clanship Among the Tallensi* (London, 1967), p. 1.

is or whose ambivalences these are, or that we shall be hearing this note, just about this muffled, again. "Highway 61 stretches across two hundred miles of rich black land known as the Mississippi Delta," begins William Ferris's fine book of a few years ago on Black musicians in the rural south, *Blues from the Delta*, "where mile-long rows of cotton and soybeans spread out from its pavement and surround occasional towns such as Lula, Alligator, Panther Burn, Nitta Yuma, Anguilla, Arcola, and Onward."[5] It is quite clear (even if one does not know that Ferris was born in the Delta) who has been movin' down that highway.

Getting themselves into their text (that is, representationally into their text) may be as difficult for ethnographers as getting themselves into the culture (that is, imaginatively into the culture). For some, it may be even more difficult (Gregory Bateson, whose eccentric classic, *Naven*, seems to consist mostly of false starts and second thoughts—preamble upon preamble, epilogue upon epilogue—comes to mind). But in one way or another, however unreflectively and with whatever misgivings about the propriety of it all, ethnographers all manage nevertheless to do it. There are some very dull books in anthropology, but few if any anonymous murmurs.

《》

The other preliminary question (what does an author author, or the discourse problem, as I called it) is also raised in more general form in Foucault's "What Is an Author?" essay and in Roland Barthes's (to my mind rather subtler) piece, "Authors and Writers," published about a decade earlier.[6]

Foucault puts the matter in terms of a distinction be-

[5] W. Ferris, *Blues from the Delta* (Garden City, N.Y., 1979), p. 1.
[6] R. Barthes, "Authors and Writers," in S. Sontag, ed., *A Barthes Reader* (New York, 1982), pp. 185–93.

tween those authors (most of us) "to whom the production of a text, a book, or a work can be legitimately attributed" and those rather more consequential figures who "author . . . much more than a book"; they author " . . . a theory, tradition, or discipline in which other books and authors will in turn find a place" (p. 153). He makes a number of debatable assertions about this phenomenon: that its nineteenth- and twentieth-century exemplars (Marx, Freud, and so on) are so radically different from earlier ones (Aristotle, Augustine, and so on) that they are not to be compared with them; that it doesn't occur in fiction writing; and that Galileo, Newton, or, though (perhaps wisely) he doesn't mention him, Einstein, are not properly instances of it. But that "founders of discursivity," as he well calls them, authors who have produced not just their own works but, in producing their own works, "have produced something else: the possibilities and the rules for the formation of other texts," are critical, not just to the development of intellectual disciplines, but to their very nature is, once stated, wildly obvious. "Freud is not just the author of *The Interpretation of Dreams* or *Jokes and Their Relation to the Unconscious*; Marx is not just the author of the *Communist Manifesto* or *Capital*: they both have established an endless possibility of discourse" (p. 154).

Perhaps it only seems endless; but we know what he means. Barthes's way of putting all this is to distinguish between an "author" and a "writer" (and, in another place, between a "work," which is what an "author" produces, and a "text," which is what a "writer" produces).[7] The author performs a function, he says; the writer, an activity. The author participates in the priest's role (he compares him to a Maussian witch doctor); the writer, in the clerk's. For an author,

[7] R. Barthes, "From Work to Text," in Harari, *Textual Strategies*, pp. 73–82.

"to write" is an intransitive verb—"he is a man who radically absorbs the world's *why* in a *how to write*." For a writer, "to write" is a transitive verb—he writes *something*. "He posits a goal (to give evidence, to explain, to instruct) of which language is merely a means; for him language supports a *praxis*, it does not constitute one. . . . [It] is restored to the nature of an instrument of communication, a vehicle of 'thought.' "[8]

All of this may rather remind one of the lady professor of "creative writing" in Randall Jarrell's *Pictures from an Institution*, who divided people into "authors" and "people," and the authors were people and the people weren't. But within anthropology it is hard to deny the fact that some individuals, whatever you call them, set the terms of discourse in which others thereafter move—for a while anyway and in their own manner. Our whole subject is differentiated, once one looks past the conventional rubrics of academic life, in such terms. Boas, Benedict, Malinowski, Radcliffe-Brown, Murdock, Evans-Pritchard, Griaule, Lévi-Strauss, to keep the list short, preterite, and variegated, point not just to particular works (*Patterns of Culture*, *Social Structure*, or *La Pensée Sauvage*), but to whole ways of going at things anthropological: they mark off the intellectual landscape, differentiate the discourse field. That is why we tend to discard their first names after a while and adjectivize their last ones: Boasian, or Griauliste, or, in a sardonic coinage of Talcott Parsons's (himself something of a Barthes *auteur* in sociology) that I have always rather fancied, Benedictine anthropology.

This distinction between "authors" and "writers," or in Foucault's version, founders of discursivity and producers

---

[8]Barthes, "Authors and Writers," pp. 187, 189.

of particular texts, is not, as such, one of intrinsic value. Many of those "writing" in traditions others have "authored" may quite surpass their models. Firth, not Malinowski, is probably our best Malinowskian. Fortes so far eclipses Radcliffe-Brown as to make us wonder how he could have taken him for his master. Kroeber did what Boas but promised. Nor is the phenomenon well captured in the easy notion of "school," which makes it sound like a matter of group formation, swimming together behind a lead fish, rather than what it is, a matter of genre formation, a move to exploit newly revealed possibilities of representation. Nor, finally, is it a clash of pure and absolute types. Barthes indeed ends "Authors and Writers" arguing that the characteristic literary figure of our age is a bastard type, the "author-writer": the professional intellectual caught between wanting to create a bewitching verbal structure, to enter what he calls the "theater of language," and wanting to communicate facts and ideas, to merchandise information; and indulging fitfully the one desire or the other. Whatever the case may be for properly *lettré* or properly scientific discourse, which would still seem to lean fairly definitively toward either language as praxis or language as means, anthropological discourse certainly remains poised, mule-like, between the two. The uncertainty that appears in signature terms as how far, and how, to invade one's text appears in discourse terms as how far, and how, imaginatively to compose it.

《》

Given all this, I want to take for my cases in point four quite different figures, Claude Lévi-Strauss, Edward Evan Evans-Pritchard, Bronislaw Malinowski, and Ruth Benedict, who, whatever else one might say about them, certainly are "authors" in the "intransitive" founders-of-discursivity

20

sense—scholars who have both signed their texts with a certain determination and built theaters of language in which a great number of others, more convincingly or less, have performed, are performing, and doubtless for some little while will continue to perform.

I will, in any case, deal with my exemplars rather differently, not only because they *are* rather different—Parisian mandarin, Oxford don, wandering Pole, New York intellectual—but because I want to pursue rather different issues by means of them. Lévi-Strauss, whom I discuss first, though he is the most recent, the most recondite, and, in literary terms, the most radical of the four, gets one into the subject at very high speed, particularly if one concentrates, as I shall, on that cassowary of a book, *Tristes Tropiques*. The extreme *textueliste* nature of the work, foregrounding its literariness at every opportunity, echoing other genres one after another, and fitting well no category but its own, makes it probably the most emphatically self-referring anthropological text we have, the one that absorbs the world's "why" most shamelessly into a "how to write." Further, like all of Lévi-Strauss's work, its relation to "cultural reality" (whatever that might be) is oblique, removed, and complexly tenuous, an apparent coming-near that is an actual drawing-back, so that it puts the established conceptions of the nature of ethnography into useful question. Lévi-Strauss has a distinctive way indeed of "being there." Whatever anthropologists may think of *Tristes Tropiques*—that it is a pretty tale, a revealing vision, or another example of what's gone wrong with the French—few come away from it without being at least a little bit deconstructed.

Evans-Pritchard is, of course, quite another matter: an author for whose style—assured, direct, and architectonic—that great oxymoron, "blinding clarity," seems to have been invented. An adventurer-ethnographer, moving with practiced ease within the imperialist world, as both observer and actor, he was out to make tribal society plain, visible even, like a branched tree or a cattle byre; his books but pictures of what they described, sketches from the life. That they should have become, these supposed models of what George Marcus and Dick Cushman in their review of recent experiments in anthropological writing call "ethnographic realism," some of the most puzzling texts in all anthropology—read variously and argued over incessantly, seen as high science or as high art, exalted as settled classics or as heterodox experiments, instanced by philosophers or celebrated by ecologists—but suggests that they are in their decorous way as cunning in their construction as Lévi-Strauss's, and as instructive.[9] Solid objects that dissolve under a steady gaze are no less fascinating than phantasmal ones that form, and perhaps even more disturbing.

In the case of Malinowski, I will be less concerned with the man himself, already too much written about, than with what he has wrought. Barthesian "author" of the participant observation, the "I was not only there, I was one of them, I speak with their voice" tradition of ethnographic writing (though not, of course, its first practitioner, any more than, say, Joyce was the first to use stream-of-consciousness narrative, or Cervantes picaresque), he made of ethnography an oddly inward matter, a question of self-testing and self-transformation, and of its writing a form of self-revelation. The breakdown of epistemological (and moral) confidence that, for all his outward bluster, began with him—as we can see from his more lately published *Diary*—has issued now in a similar breakdown in expositive confidence and produced

[9]G. Marcus and D. Cushman, "Ethnographies as Texts," in B. Siegel, ed., *Annual Review of Anthropology*, vol. ii (Palo Alto, Calif., 1982), pp. 25–69.

a flood of remedies, more or less desperate. The brooding note of Loring Danforth's "Introduction" (Who am I to be saying these things, by what right, and to what purpose, and how on earth can I manage honestly to say them?) is one now very widely heard, in various forms and with various intensities. Writing ethnography "from the native's point-of-view" dramatized for Malinowski his hopes of self-transcendence; for many of his most faithful descendants, it dramatizes their fears of self-deception.

Finally, in the schematic portraits and summary assessments of Benedict, yet another aspect of the self-reflexive, where-am-I, where-are-they, nature of anthropological writing emerges with a peculiar clarity: the way in which such writing about other societies is always at the same time a sort of Aesopian commentary on one's own. For an American to sum up Zunis, Kwakiutl, Dobu, or Japanese, whole and entire, is to sum up Americans, whole and entire, at the same time; to render them as provincial, as exotic, as comic, and as arbitrary as sorcerers and samurai. Benedict's famous relativism was less a philosophical position, systematically defended, or even for that matter consistently held, than it was a product of a particular way of describing others, one in which distant oddities were made to question domestic assumptions.

"Being There" authorially, palpably on the page, is in any case as difficult a trick to bring off as "being there" personally, which after all demands at the minimum hardly more than a travel booking and permission to land; a willingness to endure a certain amount of loneliness, invasion of privacy, and physical discomfort; a relaxed way with odd growths and unexplained fevers; a capacity to stand still for artistic insults, and the sort of patience that can support an endless search for invisible needles in infinite haystacks. And the authorial sort of being there is getting more difficult all the time. The advantage of shifting at least part of our attention from the fascinations of field work, which have held us so long in thrall, to those of writing is not only that this difficulty will become more clearly understood, but also that we shall learn to read with a more percipient eye. A hundred and fifteen years (if we date our profession, as conventionally, from Tylor) of asseverational prose and literary innocence is long enough.

THE WORLD IN A TEXT

How to Read 'Tristes Tropiques'

The advent of structuralism ("advent" is the proper word; it came as a sudden unriddling announced by an improbable presence) has done rather more to alter anthropology's sense of itself than its sense of its subject. Whatever becomes of circulating women, mythemes, binary reason, or the science of the concrete, the sense of intellectual importance that structuralism brought to anthropology, and most especially to ethnography—in which Lévi-Strauss once declared he had found nothing less than "the principle of all research"—will not soon disappear. The discipline had worked its way, here and there, into the general cultural life before: Eliot read Frazer; Engels read Morgan; Freud, alas, read Atkinson; and, in the United States at least, just about everybody read Mead. But nothing like the wholesale invasion of neighboring fields (literature, philosophy, theology, history, art, politics, psychiatry, linguistics, even some parts of biology and mathematics) had ever occurred. So precipitate a move from the edge of things to their center has turned greater heads than ours, and the effects—despite my irony, not altogether bad—will be with us, I think, more or less permanently.

What is most striking, however, in all of this is that, using the word in its uncensorious sense, it was an essentially rhetorical accomplishment. It was not the odd facts or the even odder explanations Lévi-Strauss brought forth that made of him (as Susan Sontag, who is in charge of such matters, called him) an intellectual hero.[1] It was the mode of discourse he invented to display those facts and frame those explanations.

The re-analysis of the Oedipus story only partly aside, the particular findings of structuralist anthropology have had scarcely more effect beyond the borders of the discipline than those of functionalism, culture and personality studies, or social evolutionism; quite possibly, even less. What changed the mind of the age, as none of those ever did, was the sense that a new language had appeared in which everything from ladies' fashions, as in Roland Barthes's *Le Système de la mode*, to neurology, as in Howard Gardner's *The Quest for Mind*, could be usefully discussed.[2] It was a cycle of terms (sign, code, transformation, opposition, exchange, communication, metaphor, metonymy, myth, . . . structure), borrowed and reworked from the lexicons of science and art alike, that defined Lévi-Strauss's enterprise for those whose interest in Australian section systems or Bororo village shapes was at best limited. More than anything else, he cleared an imaginative space that a generation of characters in search of a play rushed to occupy.

Again, I should make it clear, especially in the light of

[1] S. Sontag, "The Anthropologist as Hero," in S. Sontag, *Against Interpretation* (New York, 1961), pp. 69–81.
[2] R. Barthes, *Le Système de la mode* (Paris, 1967); H. Gardner, *The Quest for Mind: Piaget, Lévi-Strauss, and the Structuralist Movement* (New York, 1973).

26

my own admitted skepticism toward the structuralist project as a research program and my outright hostility to it as a philosophy of mind, that I regard this construction of an entire discourse realm from a standing start as a stunning achievement, altogether worthy of the attention it has received. Lévi-Strauss is clearly one of the true "authors" in anthropology—if originality be all, perhaps the truest. The fact that I myself am not attracted to write in the tradition he authored, preferring less ambitious strategies, is quite beside the point. To characterize someone as writing with world-making intent is not to accuse him; it is to situate him.

It is, at any rate, from such a perspective, appreciative and unconverted, that I want to approach Lévi-Strauss as a Barthesian "author-writer." He is, or rather his work is, a peculiarly illuminating case in point for the proposition that the separation of what someone says from how they say it—content from form, substance from rhetoric, *l'écrit* from *l'écriture*—is as mischievous in anthropology as it is in poetry, painting, or political oratory. The investigation of how a Lévi-Strauss text, or more exactly how *Tristes Tropiques*, the finest of his texts and the one that most illuminates the whole of his work, is put together takes us into some of the most intractable instabilities of what (borrowing a term, and some ideas as well, from the linguist Alton Becker) one may call text-building strategies in anthropology.[3]

Of course, the most immediate value of such a "lit-crit" approach to Lévi-Strauss is that he is very difficult to read; and not only, as has sometimes been argued, for flat-footed Anglo-Saxons. He is difficult not just in the recognized sense that his by now famous rain-forest prose—dripping with

[3]A. Becker, "Text Building, Epistemology, and Aesthetics in Javanese Shadow Theatre," in A. Becker and A. Yengoyan, eds., *The Imagination of Reality* (Norwood, N.J., 1979), pp. 211–43.

steamy metaphors, overgrown with luxuriant images, and flowered with extravagant puns ("thoughts" and "pansies," "ways" and "voices," and perhaps, considering the text at hand, even "tropes" and "tropics")—is so easy to get lost in. He is difficult in the deeper and more serious sense that although, stylistic extravagances aside, his books look like ordinary anthropological works, even at times like rather old-fashioned ones, Bureau of American Ethnography monographs reincarnated, they are not. They are another genre under the sun. To approach *Tristes Tropiques* with reading habits formed by experience with *We, the Tikopia* or *Patterns of Culture* or even with what might seem a better model but is really a worse one, *The Golden Bough*, is rather like the little old lady in the Thurber vignette who found *Macbeth* lacking as a detective story because it was clear whodunit from quite early on.

But the main reason for regarding Lévi-Strauss in a literary way is not the exegetical one, structuralism made easy, but that his works, and *Tristes Tropiques* most particularly, form excellent cases upon which to train such a regard.

The innocence about text-building that I ascribed to our profession in general in the last chapter certainly does not apply to him. Were he any more self-conscious, he would transport to a higher plane. In the whole of anthropology there are no works more self-referential—works that point as often to themselves as artifacts, and deliberately, as they do to what they are ostensibly about—than *Tristes Tropiques*. It is a classic example of the book whose subject is in great part itself, whose purpose is to display what, were it a novel, we would call its fictionality; a painting, its planarity; a dance, its comportment: its existence as a made thing.

If one reads, say, Meyer Fortes's *The Tallensi* or E. E. Evans-Pritchard's *The Nuer*, one can and usually does feel that one is looking through a crystal window to the reality beyond. The devices, the construction scars, the brush marks are all more or less invisible, at least to the unwary eye. In *Tristes Tropiques* (and for that matter in *La Pensée sauvage* and *Mythologiques* as well) the devices are foregrounded, pointed at, flourished even. Lévi-Strauss doesn't want the reader to look through his text, he wants him to look at it. And once one has, it is very hard ever again to look through, at least with the old epistemological nonchalance, anyone else's.

What is critical, however, is that such a how-is-this-text-built approach to *Tristes Tropiques* leads on to a some-what unstandard interpretation of Lévi-Strauss's work, both of the parts that make it up and of the by now largely un-folded totality those parts constitute. Or to put the matter less generally, we can counterpose to the two approaches usually taken to the *oeuvre entière* a third one that gives to that *oeuvre*, and thus at least indirectly to structuralism, a rather different look. Tracing out the strategies of so strateg-ical a book is not (to employ a familiar libel) just a literary ex-ercise. It is a revisionary one.

《》

Of the two usual approaches to Lévi-Strauss's work as a whole, the more common, because it seems so simple and familiar to historicistic Westerners, is to see it as a linear de-velopment: a view Lévi-Strauss himself, as a bit of deliberate mystification in my opinion, considering his famous hostil-ity to all forms of historicism, has in fact promoted.

This view is, as linear views tend to be, essentially a Whiggish one. The great structuralist enterprise begins with *Les Structures élémentaires de la parenté* in that most stan-dard of anthropological domains, kinship, in which it makes its first real, halting steps. But it is mired down by the social

THE WORLD IN A TEXT

actuality of it all: the mind sunk in materialities. Then, the story goes, in "The Structural Study of Myth" and in *Totemism*, it begins to shake free of this social dross to get more directly at its proper subject, the formal play of the human intellect. This approach is then codified, systematized, and turned into a veritable science, like Marxism, geology, or psychoanalysis, in *La Pensée sauvage*; after which it is carried to triumphant culmination in the great four-volume record of the mind gamboling freely in the fields of its own imagery, *Mythologiques*.

It would take us too far from our subject to trace out here the difficulties of this view of Lévi-Strauss's work as describing a rise from nature to culture, behavior to thought, matter to mind. It is actually plausible only so long as one doesn't look too closely into chronology or, even more importantly, into the intertextual relations that actually obtain, independently of sequence, among the various works. *Les Structures élémentaires*, with its tracing of logical transformations across vast geographic spaces, stands in many ways closer to *Mythologiques*, two decades further on, than does *La Pensée sauvage*, with its theoretical cavalry charges, methodological set pieces, and *Rive Gauche* quarrels, which was published only a year or two earlier than *Mythologiques*. One of his most recent books, *La Voie des masques*, a sort of tailpiece to the *Mythologiques*, was published in 1979 but conceived in 1943, before his first one, *La Vie familiale et sociale des Indiens Nambikwara*. And his whole argument is, in bare-bones terms, already there in the thirty pages or so of "The Structural Study of Myth," written in the 1950's. The rest is an enormous footnote.

Because the problems of Whiggism in connection with so achronic a writer as Lévi-Strauss are, once one gets down to cases, so obvious (even his individual books do not march directionally through their subjects like proper monographs, beginning at the beginning and ending at the end, but circle, hovering, around them like avian meditations, remote and brooding), another approach to his work has seemed to a number of people more promising. This is to see it, so to speak, recursively, each phase of it, or even each work, being concerned with training the constant, unchanging, structuralist gaze on one or another domain of anthropological research; a huge rotating searchlight, lighting up first this dark corner, then the next.

In this story, Lévi-Strauss, fixed of mind and sure of purpose, scatters one after another the academic ideologies blocking his path. *Les Structures élémentaires* takes on the Warner / Radcliffe-Brown / Murdock kinship controversy, displacing the whole axis of dispute. *Totemism* upends Durkheimianism and Radcliffe-Brown's vulgarization of it. *La Pensée sauvage* tilts with Sartre, epistemology, and the idea of history. *Mythologiques* dismantles and reassembles, bricoleur-style, the Boas/Müller/Frazer schedule of issues. And the rhetoric of the argument shifts appropriately as the wheel of attention turns. It is Maussian (men communicating through gifts of women) in the Australian–Southeast Asian work. It is British functionalist (though with the signs changed, "good to think rather than good to eat") in *Totemism*. It is trans-Marxist and high-linguisticist (*imagines mundi* and animal metonyms) in *La Pensée sauvage*. And it is a melange of aestheticism ("overture," "coda," "the bird nester's aria," "the fugue of the five senses," "opossum's cantata") and Enlightenment encyclopedism (ARAWAK to ZAPOTEC) in *Mythologiques*.

I won't go, here, into the problems of this approach either. It is better in some ways than the first (at least it avoids the myth of progress). It is worse in others (complete stability in the structuralist program from 1949 to 1979 is, to put it mildly, difficult to establish). The critical point is that, as my failure to mention it in describing them suggests, both approaches have difficulty accommodating *Tristes Tropiques* at all. It seems like a mere sport, even an embarrassment: a reflective, rather pointless pause in the long march toward intellective purity in the linear case; a mere personal expression, an indulgence best overlooked, in the recursive one. As I have pronounced it the key work, the center around which the whole pivots, I need to take a quite different tack.

To my mind, Lévi-Strauss's work is organized neither linearly, a progress of views, nor quantumly, a series of discontinuous reformulations of a fixed and single view; rather, it is organized, if you will, centrifugally. It is possible, I think, and profitable as well, to look at all of Lévi-Strauss's works, except *Tristes Tropiques*, even those works which, in publication terms anyway, predate it, as partial unpackings of it, developments of particular strains present, embryonically at least and usually much more fully than that, in this, the most multiplex of his writings.

Whether or not this cosmic egg view of *Tristes Tropiques* is the last word on the subject is surely debatable; but not, I should think, until it is first explored. Looking at *Tristes Tropiques* in text-building terms as the arch-text out of which the other texts are, in a logical sense, generated— Stevens's "parakeet of parakeets that above the forest of parakeets prevails / a pip of life amid a mort of tails"—can lead one into a better grasp of Lévi-Strauss's thought than can seeing it either as an advancing series of etherealizing visions or as a static and obsessive iterating theme.

《》

From this perspective the first thing to be said about *Tristes Tropiques*, and in some ways the last as well, is that it is several books at once, several quite different sorts of texts superimposed one upon the other to bring out an overall pattern, rather like a moiré.

"Superimposed" is, however, not exactly the right word. For what we have in *Tristes Tropiques* is not a hierarchical, surface-to-depth arrangement of texts, the one hidden beneath the other, so that interpretation consists in deeper penetration as one strips away the layers. What we have is co-occurring, competing, even sometimes mutually interfering texts existing at the same level.

The book is a virtual analogue of Lévi-Strauss's kaleidoscope image of "concrete thought": a syntactic conjunction of discrete elements, played out horizontally along what Roman Jakobson called the plane of contiguity, rather than a paradigmatic hierarchy of continuate elements, played out vertically on what he called the plane of similarity.[4] *Tristes Tropiques* is an ideal-typical Russian/Czech formalist poem: meaning constructed by projecting the analog axis of paradigmatic substitution, Jakobson's "metaphor," onto the digital one of syntactic combination, his "metonymy." It is, to put it more casually, and in a language less special, a manifold text *par excellence*: several books at once all jammed together to produce . . . well, we shall come back to what is produced later. First, it is necessary to look at the component elements, the thin books wildly signaling to get out inside this fat one.

In the first place, it is, of course, and despite the ironic and self-reflexive denial of the famous opening passage, a travel book in a very recognizable genre. I went here, I went there; I saw this strange thing and that; I was amazed, bored, excited, disappointed; I got boils on my behind, and

[4]R. Jakobson, "Closing Statements: Linguistics and Poetics," in T. Sebeok, ed., *Style in Language* (Cambridge, Mass., 1960), pp. 350–77.

once, in the Amazon . . . —all with the implicit undermes-
sage: Don't you wish you had been there with me or could
do the same?

An invitation to dreams of adventure and escape, and
even a dream itself. He can be as superior as he wants to be
about lantern-slide lectures, stories about the ship's dog, or
descriptions of seagulls swirling about; but just listen to him
on Fort de France:

When the clocks struck two in the afternoon Fort de France was a
dead town. There was no sign of life in the oval-bordered "main
square," which was planted with palm-trees and overrun with ram-
pant weeds—a patch of dead ground, one would have thought, in
which someone left behind a statue of Josephine Tascher de la
Pagerie, later Beauharnais. [That is Napoleon's Josephine, of
course.] No sooner had the Tunisian and I checked into the de-
serted hotel than, still shaken by the events of the morning, we
hired a car and set off toward the Lazaret, with the intention of
comforting our companions and, more especially, two young German women who had led us to believe, during the voyage out, that
they would be unfaithful to their husbands just as soon as they
could get properly cleaned up. From this point of view, the business of the Lazaret was yet another disappointment to us.[5]

Which is both crude enough and sufficiently arch for any
lantern lecture.

Or hear him, even, much further on, approach the
Tupi-Kawahib across the mid-Amazon plateau:

I had left Cuiba in June, and it was now September. For three
months I had wandered across the Plateau, camping with the Indians while my animals had a rest, or pushing on interminably

[5]C. Lévi-Strauss, *A World on the Wane*, John Russell, trans. (New York,
1961), p. 31. Although Lévi-Strauss prefers the Weightmans' translation (*Tristes Tropiques*, John and Doreen Weightman, trans. [Harmondsworth, Eng., 1976]), and it
is somewhat more accurate, I will for the most part use the Russell, because it seems
to me to bring the tone of the French better into English. In any case, I shall also
give at each citation both the Weightman reference (here, p. 32) and that in the
original (*Tristes Tropiques* [Paris, 1955], here, p. 17).

from one point to the next, asking myself the while what it would all add up to in the end. Meanwhile the jerky motion of the mule gave me sore places so atrociously painful, and yet so familiar, that I ended up by feeling they were a permanent part of my anatomy and I should even miss them if they were not there the next morning. Boredom got the upper hand of adventure. For weeks on end the same austere savannah would unroll before me—a land so dry that living plants could scarcely be distinguished from the dead stumps that marked the place where someone had lately struck camp. And as for the blackened remains of bush-fires, they seemed merely the culmination of a territory where it was the destiny of everything, sooner or later, to be burnt to a cinder.[6]

"My Life Among the Headhunters" or "Two Years in Darkest Africa" could hardly be better, or worse, than this Richard Burton / T. E. Lawrence sort of tone. Actually, there are French referents for this that would be more appropriate. The Third Republic *haute vulgarisation* popular culture was pockmarked with this sort of thing: Gide's *Voyages au Congo*, the intensely read romantic travelogues of Pierre Loti, or even such a classic mandarin figure as André Malraux, at least in his archaeological–Far Eastern phase, seem the prototypes of the attitude, and the style, Lévi-Strauss is adopting here. A systematic attempt to connect *Tristes Tropiques* with the French travel literature he was supposedly reacting against, though actually reincarnating, and even exploiting, could be extremely revealing.

In any case, whatever the models, the image of the hardy traveler, sorely beset but terribly *interested*, never leaves the book, and it connects his account to a type of social consciousness—vulgar in the root, not the tendentious, sense of the word—that this almost classic *normalien* (even though he was, as he very carefully points out in *Tristes Tropiques*, by his own choice, not literally one) would never ad-

[6]Russell, p. 313 (Weightman, p. 419; original, p. 341).

mit to and indeed has spent much of his career distancing himself from.

Second, the book is, however oddly looking a one, an ethnography. A controversial ethnography perhaps, and more than a bit over-focused; but the affirmed and affirmed pose of the ethnographer, like the disclaimed and disclaimed one of the tourist, never leaves the book. Indeed it often becomes, in its shrill insistence, a bit thick:

An antinomy, therefore, which we have as a profession on the one hand, and on the other an ambiguous enterprise, oscillating between a mission and a refuge, hearing within itself elements of both and yet always recognizably one rather than the other. Anthropology has in all this an especially favored place. It represents the second alternative [that is, the "refuge"] in its most extreme form. The ethnographer, while in no wise abdicating his own humanity, strives to know and estimate his fellowman from a lofty and distant point of vantage: only thus can he abstract them from the contingencies particular to this or that civilization. The conditions of his life and work cut him off from his own group for long periods together; and he himself acquires a kind of chronic uprootedness from the sheer brutality of the environmental changes to which he is exposed. Never can he feel himself "at home" anywhere: he will always be, psychologically speaking, an amputated man. Anthropology is, with music and mathematics, one of the few true vocations; and the anthropologist may become aware of it before ever he has been taught it.[7]

The anthropologist, as here, venturing where lesser souls—his cafe intellectual friends in Paris; the orchid-elite of French-Quarter São Paolo; his shallow, novelty-pursuing Brazilian students; and you, dear chemist, philosopher, or art historian, enfolded in your laboratory, study, or museum—dare not go, and penetrating forms of existence they can only read about: this note too runs continuously

[7]Russell, p. 58 (Weightman, pp. 66–67; original, pp. 46–47).

36

through the book. The mystique of field work that Malinowski founded and Mead proclaimed finds its apotheosis here, significantly enough in someone who has not done all that much field work and who would deny its experiential authority, as he does in *Tristes Tropiques*, as a bit of "shopgirl philosophy."

Unlike the travel text, however, which is, as such texts are by nature, one damn thing after another, the ethnographic text has a thesis, the thesis in fact that Lévi-Strauss has pursued for the quarter century or so since: namely, "the ensemble of a people's customs has always its particular style; they form into systems." The "overture" and the "coda" to *Mythologiques* are perhaps more powerful statements, "The Structural Study of Myth" a more systematic one, and the fourth chapter of *Totemism* a clearer one. But Lévi-Strauss has never been able to put capital-S Structuralism in so neat a nutshell as he was able to in *Tristes Tropiques*:[8]

The ensemble of a people's customs has always its particular style; they form into systems. I am convinced that the number of these systems is not unlimited and that human beings (at play, in their dreams, or in moments of delusion) never create *absolutely*; all they can do is to choose certain combinations from a repertory of ideas which it should be possible to reconstitute. For this one must make an inventory of all the customs which have been observed by oneself or others, the customs pictured in mythology, the customs invoked by both children and grown-ups in their games. The dreams of individuals, whether healthy or sick, should also be taken into account. With all this one could eventually establish a sort of periodical chart of chemical elements analogous to that de-

[8]Actually, in line with my argument that chronology of publication can be misleading as a guide to the development of Lévi-Strauss's ideas, the *Tristes Tropiques* formulation builds on papers published as early as 1942, passages from which are incorporated in it. It is as much a summa as it is a prolegomena, even if most of the classic texts postdate it.

vised by Mendelier. In this, all customs, whether real or merely possible, would be grouped by families and all that would remain for us to do would be to recognize those which societies had, in point of fact, adopted.[9]

Third, besides a travelogue and an ethnography, the book is a philosophical text. It is a philosophical text not simply in the man-in-the-street sense that it is flamboyantly reflective—the mute-exchanges-of-forgiveness-with-a-cat sort of thing—and full of dark sayings—"Marxism and Buddhism are doing the same thing, but at different levels." It is a philosophical text in the scholarly sense that it addresses itself, and with some resoluteness, to a central issue in Western thought: the natural foundations of human society. Not only does Lévi-Strauss hope to find Rousseau's Social Contract alive and well in deepest Amazon—and so counter such theories of the origins of sociality as Freud's primal parricide or Hume's conventionality—but he thinks that, among the Nambikwara, he has actually and literally done so:

The evidence of the Nambikwara runs, to begin with, clean counter to the ancient sociological theory, now temporarily resurrected by the psychoanalysts, according to which the primitive chief derives from a symbolic father. . . . I should like to be able to show how markedly, in this regard, contemporary anthropology supports the thesis of the eighteenth century *philosophes*. Doubtless Rousseau's schema differs from the quasi-contractual relations which obtain between the chief and his companions. Rousseau had in mind a quite different phenomenon—the renunciation by the individual of his own autonomy in the interests of the collective will. It is nonetheless true, however, that Rousseau and his contemporaries displayed profound sociological intuition when they realized that attitudes and elements of culture such as are summed up in the words "contract" and "consent" are not second-

[9]Russell, p. 160 (Weightman, p. 229; original, p. 183).

ary formations, as their adversaries (and Hume in particular) maintained: they are the primary materials of social life, and it is impossible to imagine a form of social organization in which they are not present.[10]

Lévi-Strauss does not merely think that he has found the Social Contract *in vivo* (a claim, a bit like saying one has discovered the country where Plato's Ideas or Kant's Noumena are stored). He wants to bring back to respectability Rousseau's *societé naissante* model, which sees what we would now call the neolithic as, quoting from Rousseau, "un juste milieu entre l'indolence d'état primitif et la pétulant activité de notre amour propre" ("the middle ground between the indolence of the primitive state and the questing activity to which we are prompted by our *amour propre*"). Better we had never left that world, which we need now to reconstruct, and which we can reconstruct because Rousseau's model is eternal and universal.[11] By knowing other societies, we can detach ourselves from our own and build, on the basis of an ideal beyond space and time, a rational social order, one, Lévi-Strauss says, in which man can live.

And this, in turn, leads to the fourth sort of text *Tristes Tropiques* is: a reformist tract. There has been an enormous number of indictments by now of the West for its impact on the non-West, but there are few, no matter how radical their authors, with the devastating bitterness and power of Lévi-Strauss's *Tristes Tropiques*. He makes Franz Fanon sound positively genial.

The passages are famous. The descriptions of the dilap-

[10] Russell, p. 308 (Weightman, pp. 313–14; original, p. 336). For more on this theme in Lévi-Strauss's work generally, see C. Geertz, "The Cerebral Savage" in C. Geertz, *The Interpretation of Cultures* (New York, 1973), pp. 345–59.

[11] Russell, p. 390 (Weightman, p. 315; original, p. 513).

idated "former savages" spoiling the view around São Paolo; the diatribes about empty beer bottles and discarded tin cans; and the intense hatred for industrial civilization that keeps breaking through: it is unnecessary to requote them here. What needs to be noted is that they connect with a distinctive strand in nineteenth- and early twentieth-century reformist thought—the one perhaps best represented in France by Flaubert, in Germany by Nietzsche, and by Arnold or Ruskin or Pater in England; one that reacted to much of modern life with an essentially aesthetic repugnance raised, or anyway transported, to a moral level. Distaste transmogrified.

Just to show that this is a general theme in Lévi-Strauss, let me quote from his comments on Third-World cities, describing them as a whole. (The passage, revamped and back-translated for Indian cities expressly, is in fact included in *Tristes Tropiques*, though it is one of the sections omitted in the Russell translation): "Filth, promiscuity, disorder, physical contact; ruins, shacks, excrements, mud; body moisture, animal droppings, urine, purulence, secretions, suppuration—everything that [European] urban life is organized to defend us against, everything we loathe, everything we protect ourselves from at great cost—all these by-products of co-habitation never here [in the Third World] impose a limit on [urban life's] spread. On the contrary, these constitute the natural setting the town must have if it is to survive."[12]

And the crime, of course, is that it is we who have done this, whether out of greed and *pétulant activité* or mere fits of absentmindedness and callousness—we who have thrown, as he says somewhere in *Tristes Tropiques*, our

[12]I have been unable to recover the Lévi-Strauss passage in English. It appears in Weightman at p. 168; in the original at p. 132.

filth in the faces of the rest of the world, which now proceeds to throw it back in ours.

As a reformist tract, *Tristes Tropiques* is an outburst, less of *moraliste* rage—which is one of the things that divides him from Sartre, who is rather more worried that people are dominated than that they are degraded—than of aesthetic repugnance. Like Swift's, Lévi-Strauss's deep social disgust seems to rise out of an even deeper disgust with the physical and the biological. His radicalism is not political. It is sensory.

Fifth, and finally, *Tristes Tropiques* is, and quite deliberately, a kind of symbolist literary text (a fact James Boon, in his neglected study, *From Symbolism to Structuralism*, has alerted us to in Lévi-Strauss's work generally),[13] an application of *symboliste* views to primitive culture: Mallarmé in South America.

This is easier to see in the French text, where the prose as such mirrors the indebtedness. But it is emphatic enough at various points to survive translation as well:

I see these predilections [to see space and time in qualitative terms, and so on] as a form of wisdom which primitive peoples put simultaneously into practice; the madness lies rather in our modern wish to go against them. Primitive peoples attained quickly and easily to a peace of mind which we strive for at the cost of innumerable rebuffs and irritations. We should do better to accept the true conditions of our human experience and realize that it is not within our power to emancipate ourselves completely from either its structure or its natural rhythms. Space has values peculiar to itself, just as sounds and scents have their colours and feelings their weight. The search for correspondences of this sort is not a poet's game or a department of mystification, as people have dared to say of Rimbaud's *Sonnet des Voyelles*; that sonnet is now indispensable

[13] J. Boon, *From Symbolism to Structuralism: Lévi-Strauss and Literary Tradition* (Oxford, 1972).

to the student of language who knows the basis, not of the colour of phenomena, for this varies with each individual, but of the relation which unites one phenomenon to another and comprises a limited gamut of possibilities. These correspondences offer the scholar an entirely new terrain, and one which may still have rich yields to offer. If fish can make an aesthetic distinction between smells in terms of light and dark, and bees classify the strength of light in terms of weight—darkness is heavy to them, and bright light light—just so should the work of the painter, the poet, and the composer and the myths and symbols of primitive Man appear to us: if not as a superior form of knowledge, at any rate as the most fundamental form of knowledge, and the only one that we all have in common.[14]

And he continues in the same vein, one which by *Mythologiques* will be a major theme. "Cities have often been likened to symphonies and poems; and this comparison seems to me a perfectly natural one: they are in fact objects of the same nature . . . something lived and something dreamed."[15] (Apparently these are different cities than the pestilent ones we just saw. And, in fact, this bit of lyricism is followed by a criticism of Brazilian towns, this time for being the results of "decisions of . . . engineers and financiers" rather than spontaneous growths, like poems or symphonies—unmelodic, out of tune, so to speak: mechanical cacophonies produced by tone-deaf "moderns.")

That Lévi-Strauss is concerned to place himself and his text in the literary tradition established by Baudelaire, Mallarmé, Rimbaud, and—though, as far as I can discover, he never mentions him in *Tristes Tropiques*—especially Proust, is clear from the way he writes, from what he writes, and from what he says he is concerned to do: decode, and, in decoding, recover the power to use the sensuous imagery of neolithic thought. *Tristes Tropiques* is, in one dimension, a

---

[14]Russell, pp. 126–27 (Weightman, pp. 153–54; original, p. 121).
[15]Russell, p. 127 (Weightman, p. 154; original, p. 122).

record of a symbolist mentality, which Lévi-Strauss insists that not just his Indians but he himself has, at play in the forests and savannahs of the Amazon:

Neither Brazil nor South America meant much to me at the time. But I can still see, in every detail, the images formed in my mind, in response to this unexpected suggestion [that is, that he go there]. Tropical countries, as it seemed to me, must be the exact opposite of our own, and the name of the antipodes has for me a sense at once richer and more ingenuous than its literal derivation. I should have been astonished to hear it said that any species, whether animal or vegetable, could have the same appearance on both sides of the globe. Every animal, every tree, every blade of grass, must be completely different and give immediate notice . . . of its tropical character. I imagined Brazil as a tangled mass of palm-leaves, with glimpses of strange architecture in the middle distance, and an all-permeating sense of burning perfume. This latter olefactory detail I owe, I think, to an unconscious awareness of the assonance between the words *Brésil* ("Brazil") and *grésiller* ("sizzle"). No amount of later experience . . . can prevent me from still thinking of Brazil in terms of burning scent.

Now that I look back on them, these images no longer seem so arbitrary. I have learnt that the truth of any given situation does not yield so much to day-to-day observation as that patient and fractionated distillation which the equivocal notion of burning scent was perhaps already inviting me to put into practice. The scent brought with it, it may be, a symbolic lesson which I was not yet able to formulate clearly. Exploration is not so much a matter of covering ground as of digging beneath the surface: chance fragments of landscape, momentary snatches of life, reflections caught on the wing—such are the things that alone make it possible for us to understand and interpret horizons which would otherwise have nothing to offer us.[16]

The book is a record of a symbolist mentality (French) encountering other symbolist mentalities (Bororo, Caduveo, Nambikwara) and seeking to penetrate their wholly in-

16 Russell, pp. 49–50 (Weightman, pp. 55–56; original, pp. 37–38).

terior coherence in order to find in them the replication of itself—"the most fundamental form" of thought.

As I say, only even more extended quotation could bring this fully out: the stress on the affinity of memory, music, poetry, myth, and dream; the notion of a universal *sauvage* sense-language, half buried in each person (and more deeply buried in us, who have left the *société naissante*, than in primitives); and the closed-world view of meaning that results from it all. *Tristes Tropiques* is Lévi-Strauss's *A la recherche du temps perdu* and *Un Coup de dès*, and insists on being read as such, as part of the symbolist effort to orchestrate immediate images into absolute signs—something your standard, average British or American anthropologist is not particularly well equipped, and certainly not inclined, to do.

《》

So: A travel book, even a tourist guide, if, like the tropics, out of date. An ethnographic report, founding yet one more *scienza nuova*. A philosophical discourse, attempting to rehabilitate Rousseau, the Social Contract, and the virtues of the unpetulant life. A reformist tract, attacking European expansionism on aesthetic grounds. And a literary work, exemplifying and forwarding a literary cause . . . All of these set next to one another, juxtaposed like pictures from an exhibition, producing in their interaction precisely what? What is the moiré that emerges?

To my mind what emerges, not altogether surprisingly I suppose, is a myth.[17] The encompassing form of the book that all this syntactic, metonymic jostling of text-types produces is a Quest Story: the departure from familiar, boring, oddly threatening shores; the journey, with adventures, into

[17]Again, I have developed this point more fully in "The Cerebral Savage," and so merely reassert it here.

another, darker world, full of various phantasms and odd revelations; the culminating mystery, the absolute other, sequestered and opaque, confronted deep down in the *sertão*; the return home to tell tales, a bit wistfully, a bit wearily, to the uncomprehending who have stayed unadventurously behind.

This too, of course, this Anthropologist-as-seeker myth, can be seen as just one more metonymically adjoined text, side-by-side with the others, the meaning of the whole lying in good structuralist style (thus with good structuralist elusiveness) in the conjunction rather than in the parts conjoined. What is clear, however, is that in the years since *Tristes Tropiques*—or, more exactly, after the experience that of course preceded *all* his writings—Lévi-Strauss has dedicated himself to the writing of a myth about myths that would do what the direct experiences related in *Tristes Tropiques* finally (and, in the nature of the case, inevitably) failed to do: bring together the multiple text-types into a single structure, a "mytho-logic," itself an example of its subject, and so reveal the foundations of social life, and indeed, beyond that, the foundations of human existence as such.

Seen this way, the body of Lévi-Strauss's systematic work appears as a long utterance in which the separate texts of *Tristes Tropiques* are connected and reconnected and reconnected again to one another in a grand variety of syntactic relations. If the myth-text can in any sense be said to emerge from the congeries that is *Tristes Tropiques* to dominate the whole *oeuvre* that unfolds out of it, it is as, so to speak, the syntax of syntax, the enclosing form abstract enough to represent, or better, govern, the whole. *This* is why Lévi-Strauss regards myth, music, and mathematics as the most direct expressions of reality, and their study the only true vocations. It all ends, to the extent that it can be said to end at all, in a formalist metaphysics of being, never stated but always insinuated, never written but always displayed.

But this takes us further toward interpreting Lévi-Strauss's doctrine, as opposed to investigating his discourse strategies, than it is possible to go here.[18] The critical issue, so far as concerns the anthropologist as author, works and lives, text-building, and so on, is the highly distinctive representation of "being there" that *Tristes Tropiques* develops, and the equally distinctive representation, invertive actually, of the relationship between referring text and referred-to world that follows from it.

To put it brutally, but not inaccurately, Lévi-Strauss argues that the sort of immediate, in-person "being there" one associates with the bulk of recent American and British anthropology is essentially impossible: it is either outright fraud or fatuous self-deception. The notion of a continuity between experience and reality, he says early on in *Tristes Tropiques*, is false: "there is no continuity in the passage between the two. . . . To reach reality we must first repudiate experience, even though we may later reintegrate it into an objective synthesis in which sentimentality [i.e. *sentimentalité*—"consciousness," "sensibility," "subjectivity," "feeling"] plays no part. . . . [Our] mission . . . is to understand Being in relation to itself, and not in relation to oneself."[19]

But what is most interesting is that this conviction, amounting indeed to a proper faith, that "savages" are best

[18]Though it is, of course, part of my argument (the heart of it, in fact) that the relation between the *ars intelligendi*, the art of understanding, and the *ars explicandi*, the art of presentation, is so intimate in anthropology as to render them at base inseparable. That is why to see *Tristes Tropiques* as an image of its argument is to revise our view of what that argument is.

[19]Russell, p. 62 (Weightman, p. 71; original, p. 50).

known not by an attempt to get, somehow, personally so close to them that one can share in their life, but by stitching their cultural expressions into abstract patterns of relationships, is represented in *Tristes Tropiques* as arising out of a revelatory (or, perhaps better, anti-revelatory) climactic experience: the barren, defeated end of his Quest. When, finally, he reaches the ultimate savages he has so long been looking for—the "untouched" Tupi-Kawahib—he finds them unreachable:

I had wanted to reach extreme limits of the savage; it might be thought that my wish had been granted, now that I found myself among these charming Indians whom no other white man had ever seen before and who might never be seen again. After an enchanting trip up-river, I had certainly found my savages. Alas! they were only too savage. . . . There they were . . . as close to me as a reflection in a mirror; I could touch them, but I could not understand them. I was given, at one and the same time, my reward and my punishment. . . . I had only to succeed in guessing what they were like for them to be deprived of their strangeness: in which case, I might just as well have stayed in my [own] village. Or if, as was the case here, they retained their strangeness, I could make no use of it, since I was incapable of even grasping what it consisted of. Between these two extremes, what ambiguous instances provide us [anthropologists] with the excuses by which we live? Who . . . is the real dupe of the confusion created in the reader's mind by observations which are carried just far enough to be intelligible and then are stopped in mid-career, because they cause surprise in human beings [who are] similar to those who take such customs as a matter of course? Is it the reader who believes in us, or we ourselves . . . ?[20]

The answer to this rhetorical question is, of course, both: the reader because he or she credits the anthropologist with a kind of experience the anthropologist has not in fact

---

[20]Here I have used the Weightman translation (pp. 436–37), for it is a bit clearer than the Russell (p. 327; original, pp. 356–57).

884030

had; the anthropologist because he (or she, of course) imagines he has had it, and that his having had it is what gives him his authority to speak. Seeing through to the foundations of strange-looking lives—"being there" in the general sense—cannot be achieved by personal immersion in them. It can only be achieved by subjecting the cultural productions (myths, arts, rituals, or whatever), the things that give these lives their immediate look of strangeness, to a universalizing analysis that, in dissolving the immediacy, dissolves the strangeness. What is remote close up is, at a remove, near.[21]

And this brings us, at last and at length, to the marking characteristic of all of Lévi-Strauss's work, one upon which almost everyone who deals with it sooner or later remarks: its extraordinary air of abstracted self-containment. "Aloof," "closed," "cold," "airless," "cerebral"—all the epithets that collect around any sort of literary absolutism collect around it. Neither picturing lives nor evoking them, neither interpreting them nor explaining them, but rather arranging and rearranging the materials the lives have somehow left behind into formal systems of correspondences—his books seem to exist behind glass, self-sealing discourses into which jaguars, semen, and rotting meat are admitted to become oppositions, inversions, isomorphisms.

The final message of *Tristes Tropiques*, and of the *oeuvre* that unfolds from it, is that anthropological texts, like myths and memoirs, exist less for the world than the world exists for them.

---

[21] For a vivid, and more recent, expression of his ambivalence about approaching other peoples too closely, see C. Lévi-Strauss, *The View from Afar* (New York, 1985), especially the introduction and first chapter. For an examination of some of the moral implications of this stance, see C. Geertz, "The Uses of Diversity," in S. McMurrin, ed., *The Tanner Lectures on Human Values*, vol. 7 (Cambridge, Eng., 1986), pp. 253–75.

3

SLIDE SHOW

Evans-Pritchard's African Transparencies

There are some voices that are very easy to imitate, whether for mockery or social climbing, but are almost impossible to describe, so particularly inflected, exactly displaced, precisely off-common are they. The East Indian manner in English is perhaps one such; so is Humphrey Bogart's or Louis Armstrong's or Franklin Roosevelt's. They linger in the auditory memory: once heard, exasperatingly difficult to forget. Among those that have been significant in anthropology, that of the Oxbridge Senior Common Room is far and away the most important, and there has been no greater master of it than Sir Edward Evan Evans-Pritchard: "E-P."

Because it is so difficult, especially as a written style, to characterize—such adjectives as "assured," "limpid," "measured," "equanimous," "effortless," "superior," "conversational" but beat around its edges—it is necessary to quote a fair patch of the stuff to convey the maddening brilliance of it. Almost any line of E-P, stylistically one of the most homogeneous writers the world has seen, would do—from the opening one of his first major work, the 1937 *Witchcraft, Or-*

acles, and Magic Among the Azande ("If I seem to have been overlong in publishing a monograph on Zande culture I would plead that I have done my best to write preliminary and partial accounts of Zande customs during the intervals between my expeditions"), to the last of his last, the 1956 *Nuer Religion* ("At this point the theologian takes over from the anthropologist").[1] But rather than quote from any of his anthropological writings—more than 350 items, including five major works—I want to take us into his prose world by means of some fairly extended excerpts from a fugitive, out-of-category, little-noticed piece in which he describes his activities as a bush-irregular in the Sudan during the early phases of the Second World War: "Operations on the Akobo and Gila Rivers, 1940–41," published in *The Army Quarterly*, a British military journal, in 1973, the last year of his life.[2]

I do this not to be perverse or cute, nor to unmask him as possessed (as he certainly was, and even defiantly) of a colonial mentality—let him who writes free of his time's imaginings cast the first stone—but because the piece, some nine printed pages overall, displays virtually all the characteristics of E-P's way with discourse in a text in which his substantive and methodological arguments as an anthropologist do not, save glancingly, figure. Much as *Tristes Tropiques* for Lévi-Strauss (though the two discourses differ radically in just about every other possible way, including their importance, central in the one case, trivial in the other, in the overall

[1] E. E. Evans-Pritchard, *Witchcraft, Oracles, and Magic Among the Azande* (Oxford, 1937), p. 1; *Nuer Religion* (New York, 1956), p. 322.

[2] E. E. Evans-Pritchard, "Operations on the Akobo and Gila Rivers, 1940-41," *The Army Quarterly*, 103, no. 4 (July 1973): 1–10. For a general discussion of Evans-Pritchard's rather intricate relations with the British government in the Sudan from 1928 on, see P. H. Johnson, "Evans-Pritchard, the Nuer, and the Sudan Civil Service," *African Affairs*, 81 (1982): 231–46.

canon), "Operations on the Akobo" gives a nutshell image of the limits of E-P's discourse that are, as are anyone's, the Wittgensteinian limits of his world.

But apologies are easy, especially for sins not yet committed; let us get on with it. E-P, then 37 and in the Middle of the Journey, both in career and in life, was posted, so the Major-General who introduces the Akobo piece to its military audience instructs us, to one of the least-known parts of what was then the frontier between Italian-occupied and British-held territories in East Africa, six hundred miles south of Khartoum, four hundred north of Lake Rudolf, five hundred west of Addis Ababa. E-P himself relates, with customary briskness, how this came to happen in his opening passage:

Perhaps I should begin by explaining how I became caught up in the events I describe. When war broke out I was at the time a Lecturer in Oxford University and I made an attempt to join the Welsh Guards. The regiment accepted me but I was prevented from training by the University on the grounds—pointless as it seemed to me—that I was in a "reserved occupation." So I went to the Sudan on the excuse of continuing my ethnographical researches there and on arrival joined the Sudan Auxiliary Defence Force. This was just what I wanted and what I could do, for I had made researches in the Southern Sudan for some years and spoke with ease some of its languages, including Nuer and Anuak. (p. 2)

He had, uniquely, ethnographically, "been there," and once there again his expertise came rapidly into play:

Captain Lesslie [the Royal Scots officer in command of the sector, whom, E-P manages to make clear, he did not much care for] attached me to the Gila Force, with instructions to patrol the upper Akobo river and keep an eye on the Anuak of the Adongo region, for no one knew what was happening there. I should explain at this point . . . that the Anuak are a Nilotic people, on a rough estimate 35,000 in number, living along rivers in the Sudan and

Ethiopia. They are almost entirely agricultural, tsetse fly preventing the keeping of cattle in most of their country. They have somewhat complicated social and political institutions, and all that need be said here is that in the eastern . . . part of their country, where the minor operations about to be described took place, there is a king, who keeps his preeminence so long as he can retain the royal emblems. If a noble kinsman attacks him and can deprive him of them he loses his crown to the attacker. The . . . Anuak country is remote and difficult to reach, and it can scarcely be said to have been administered . . . in more than name, either by the Anglo-Egyptian . . . or the Ethiopian Government[s]; and its people are warlike and independent. (p. 2)

Arrived, signed on, his bona fides presented, he collects his guns and his natives and is away immediately from parade-ground captains to the liberty of the bush:

At Akobo I was issued with fifteen rifles of a last century model and 50 rounds apiece, and told to recruit a force of irregulars from among the Anuak. I took with me . . . seven of the local Anuak as I knew the men personally, though I had little confidence that they would remain with me for long. I decided to recruit the other eight from the . . . Anuak to the east because they knew the area in which we were to operate, had more sense of discipline than the local[s], and had some regard for the opinion of the man who at that time was the Anuak king. . . . Fortunately all Anuak could handle rifles and were fairly accurate shots at very close range, and they did not object to living on the country. With so small a force everything obviously depended on mobility and good intelligence. We moved mostly at night as is the Anuak custom in war. I had the great advantage of having been through the country before . . . and of knowing also the people and their language. I gave a very liberal interpretation to my instructions. (pp. 2–3)

Both British and an anthropologist, E-P heads, like Firth in Tikopia, directly for that king (though it is the rainy season and the route is largely under water), who is very glad to see him, "for he thought that the Italians would be persuaded by his kinsman and rival . . . who lived in Ethiopia, to attack him and seize the Anuak royal emblems" (p. 3). E-P recruits eight "lads" from the king's homestead, including the king's brother, later king himself, and sets off to conduct his "minor operations":

[On 6 November] I started with my force of fifteen Anuak for the upper Akobo. We got through the swamps and high grasses with the utmost difficulty. I received a warm welcome from the inhabitants of these upstream villages for they remembered me well from my earlier visit. [We intended] to return downstream on the following day, but we learnt that there was a small picquet from the Boma force at Ukwaa. I sent a message to it saying I intended to pay a visit next day, but shortly after the message had gone I received intelligence that an Italian force was advancing toward Ukwaa to attack the picquet so I left for the village at once, arriving opposite it about midnight. The picquet's information, later confirmed from Italian sources, was that a force of native irregulars with a good number of Somali regulars under two Italian officers, probably round about 200 strong, was just outside the village near a rock called Abula, a well-known Anuak landmark. I told the picquet to evacuate Ukwaa and join me on the Sudan side of the river. (p. 3)

He attempts at first to ambush the Italian force, all two hundred of them, and, when that fails, he trails it as it moves back and forth along the opposite bank, exchanging a few shots now and then. Tiring of this, "the Italians sent a message to say that if we did not clear off they would attack us. I sent back a suitable reply." The greater part of the Italian force then departs for its base, leaving a detachment of thirty men or so on the Akobo, which E-P and his band of fifteen promptly attack. "There was much wild rifle fire and from the Italian side some machine-gunning and throwing of hand grenades, the total result of which was one Italian casualty. They reported this as an important engagement.

They packed up at once . . . and we never saw them again"
(p. 4).

His force exhausted from trekking about in the rain on
insufficient food and himself down with fever, E-P estab-
lishes a camp alongside the river—a break in the action that
is matched with one in the narrative as he reflects on the sort
of men he was leading and on his manner of leading them:

I may say here something of the qualities of the Anuak as fighters.
They are brave, but become very excited and expose themselves
unnecessarily. They like to fire from the hip and when firing from
the shoulder do not use the sights, so to conduct a successful skirmish it is necessary to take them right up to the enemy and let
them shoot at point-blank range. They must be led. They will go
with you anywhere and will not desert you in a scrap if things go
badly, but they will not go without you. I found too that it was
necessary to consult them before any action and to lead by example
rather than by command, for they are rugged individuals and very
obstinate. I learnt that if, after discussion of the course of action I
proposed they refused to agree to it, I could attain my object by
proceeding to carry out the proposed operation myself, where-
upon all eventually followed suit. (p. 4)

Soon recovered, E-P wants to take his little band, now
risen to a couple of dozen, and capture the Italians—several
hundred strong—at their headquarters at Agenga, so as "to
break [their] prestige on the Gila." ("I was confident that
Agenga could be taken by surprise without much loss of
life.") But Lesslie forbids it, sending E-P a few Anuak foot-
police "to compensate me for my disappointment." A few
days later, some local Anuak tell him that about thirty men
from Agenga under an Ethiopian NCO have entered a
nearby village:

This seemed too good an opportunity to be missed. I sent my Anuak to start an attack on the village on the land side while I and the

foot-police moved up to it on the river side. The enemy had the advantage of the village ramparts and were assisted by the Anuak population of the village. My Anuak drew enemy fire and enabled the police and myself to get close to the village without being spotted. They afterwards worked round the village to join us in a frontal attack. We crawled under heavy but very wild fire to go within point-blank range. Some of my Anuak got into the village and fired the huts and in the confusion created . . . we rushed the position. We had contacted the enemy at 7:30 in the morning and took the village just three hours later. Enemy casualties were eight dead and two wounded. We had no casualties. The Italians reported they had been attacked by fifty [colonial soldiers] and 250 Anuak. . . . The taking of [the village] was a blow to Italian prestige in that part of Anuakland where it was the strongest [and] an encouragement to our supporters among the Anuak, especially as in Anuak fighting among themselves the great object is to take a village from its defenders and destroy it, as we had done. (pp. 4–5)

I will not follow the story of E-P's adventures any further, though the Black-and-White-in-Color charm of it all makes it difficult to resist. The tone, which is what I am after, should be clear, and I will just append, *presto staccato*, a few more disconnected quotations concerning his view of the Anuak and of himself among them, to round out the picture; for, indeed, a picture is precisely what we have here: *Images Afriques*.

Thus, on the inability of the Italians, who had heard that an Englishman, "Udier Uscian" ("my Anuak name was Odier wa Cang"), was in the area but could learn nothing about him, to get information from the Anuak:

The Anuak did not like the Italians even though many of them took Italian pay and joined their irregular bands, and they let my force through their country without warning the enemy, whereas the slightest move in our direction was at once reported, the civilian population acting as self-appointed scouts, sentinels and spies.

The Italians tried to get information by threats and promises of rewards and only got nonsense. They did not know how to obtain information from the people by treating them decently. (p. 6)

On the difficulty of disciplining the Anuak ("who were prepared to march and fight but not just to march") when away from an immediate scene of action:

On the way I had the worst trouble I ever had with the Anuak. They said they were completely fed up with this constant marching about the countryside to no purpose and would not go to Gila again unless I could promise them that there would be a fight when they got there. For security I felt I could not tell them about [a planned air attack there]. Finally I told them that they could come with me . . . or not as they pleased but that I was going there in any case. In the end they followed. (p. 6)

On the Anuak's courage in action, when properly led:

For some reason . . . the Italian officer in charge of this detachment withdrew after a short skirmish and left the garrison [Galla tribesmen from southern Ethiopia] to its fate. We killed seventeen irregular troops . . . and wounded a considerable number of those who got away. Unfortunately five women, wives of Galla, and a child, who were in the trenches were killed also. Two of my Anuak were wounded . . . when we charged the trenches. The Anuak had fought very courageously. They were a dreadful nuisance most of the time but they were good to have around in a fight. (p. 7)

And on the superiority of British (never mind Italian) officers, who understand the natives, over those who do not:

Lesslie and I did not see eye to eye about the best way of attacking the post. The Anuak, whose point of view I expressed, thought the venture was a bad bet but that it might come off if we approached the enemy position by night and attacked at dawn, extending when the fighting began. Lesslie wanted to act more in accordance with textbook tactics and attack by daylight. As he was in command we had to do things his way. (p. 8)

This, of course, ended badly, and the Anuak, "who protested strongly," were ordered to withdraw. The center sections "who had no British officer with them . . . bolted," and the British were surrounded. "Without the Anuak we would, I think, have been lost, but following their guidance we bolted into the long grass away from the river and taking our wounded with us [escaped]" (p. 8). Lesslie himself is killed, we are informed in a clause, a short time later; but the Italians are finally cleared out of the Akobo-Gila area, and E-P, tired, three stone lighter, and plagued by unhealing wounds, is dispatched, against his inclinations, on a six-weeks march up the Gila into Ethiopia to demonstrate British domination: "My instructions were to show the flag so I decided to do so in the most literal sense. My column was preceded on the march by a large Union Jack at the end of a pole, and this was planted in all the villages where we camped" (p. 10).

They are, as usual, glad to see him wherever he goes—save in the village where the Italian headquarters had been, where the people flee into the bush. "Coming back through the swamps," he concludes his tale, in his finest Boy's Own Book manner, "was a real hard job, but on the whole the trip was interesting" (p. 10).

《》

It would be as unwise to assume that Evans-Pritchard was anything less than intensely aware of the figure he is cutting here as it would be to swallow him or his story whole. The tale has clearly been through too many pub recitals to be the offhand account it so industriously pretends to be. What is interesting is how that effect, something common to all of E-P's work, whatever the subject or the intent, is accomplished, and why—why, authorially—it is sought. His easy

certitude of perception is a difficult thing to bring off rhetorically—at least as difficult as Lévi-Strauss's Gongorism,
and perhaps more so—especially when one is dealing, as
E-P was and knew that he was, throughout his whole career with precisely the sort of materials that most gravely
challenge it. It is one thing to write about the fenced-off gardens of English poetry in sentences that all end—as Denis
Donoghue has written with respect to another votary of this
sidelong approach to prose, Dame Helen Gardner—with an
implied "of course."[3] It is quite another to write in such sentences about witchcraft or anarchy or scrambling around minor tributaries of the White Nile with pigheaded Scotsmen,
clownish Italians, and mercurial Blacks.

It is, as well, very difficult—simply because they are so
backgrounded, so blended into the familiar between-us hum
of educated speech—to isolate the means by which this in
fact quite elaborate text-building strategy is pursued. But
clearly this strategy rests most fundamentally on the existence of a very strictly drawn and very carefully observed
narrative contract between writer and reader. The presump-
tions that connect the author and his audience, presump-
tions that are social, cultural, and literary at once, are so
strong and so pervasive, so deeply institutionalized, that
very small signals can carry very big messages. As Donoghue
goes on to say, *in re* Dame Helen and what he calls more
generally "gunboat linguistics":

The reader doesn't need to have the point explained, a nod will do,
and he's expected to be gratified by the evidence that he's deemed
worthy of this attention. The sentence has the inflection of a
glance. It helps, if the writer is an Oxford don; better still if he
gives the impression of being such a person by birth, class, nature,
and nurture, as well as by notable academic achievement and the

[3]D. Donoghue, *Ferocious Alphabets* (Boston, 1981), p. 12.

publication of such a work as the one the reader is now holding. Then you can appeal to shared values, good taste, fine discernment, which make communication a privilege congenially offered and accepted.[4]

I must say immediately, in line with my anxiety not to be seen as seeking to unmask, demystify, deconstruct, or otherwise belittle my "authors," all of whom, including E-P, I hold in high regard, whatever our differences in social attitudes, that I do not share Donoghue's cheerfully admitted Irishman's dislike of this mode of discourse (though I see what he means about Dame Helen, who has raised the preemptive "We" to unsuspected heights). Indeed, it seems to me a "theatre of language" of enormous power—in ethnography, the most powerful yet constructed. Certainly, with the appearance of the so-called British "school" of social anthropology, which is held together far more by this manner of going about things in prose than it is by any sort of consensual theory or settled method, it has become the most prominent. (What E-P, A. R. Radcliffe-Brown, Meyer Fortes, Max Gluckman, Edmund Leach, Raymond Firth, Audrey Richards, S. F. Nadel, Godfrey Lienhardt, Mary Douglas, Emrys Peters, Lucy Mair, and Rodney Needham share, aside from rivalry, is tone—though, naturally, some of them are greater masters of it than others.) Even most Americans sound, by now, a bit like "Operations on the Akobo."

In any case, no matter how carefully the species markings of this sort of "of-course" discourse are camouflaged by a studied air of unstudiedness (that is one of the major markings: everything—those Galla women and children, for example—is too casual by half), once one realizes that

[4]Donoghue, *Ferocious Alphabets*, pp. 12–13. The "gunboat linguistics" comment is at p. 30.

they are in fact there, they are not all that difficult to spot. Some, like the extreme simplicity and regularity of sub-sentence punctuation (as few commas as possible, mechanically placed, and hardly any semicolons at all: readers are expected to know when to breathe), are only visible in the written texts. Others, like the related avoidance of clause embedding, amounting almost to a phobia, can perhaps be sensed even aurally. (In the writing there is a dash or a parenthesis now and then, but they are also rare, as are colons, apart from their use in introducing quoted text.) The passion for simple subject-predicate-object sentences, unmodified and undecorated, is intense. ("For you," as Clemenceau is supposed to have instructed his amanuensis, "there are only nouns and verbs; I will take care of such adjectives as may prove necessary.") Though E-P spoke at least French and Italian fluently, there are virtually no foreign phrases, aside, of course, from native vernacular, in his ethnographic writings. Though he was very broadly educated, literary allusions play little role. And though he was the professional's professional in self-presentation, the absence of jargon, anthropological or any other, is so nearly total as to seem ostentatious. The only speech act of any frequency is the flat declarative. Quizzical interrogatives, hedging conditionals, musing apostrophes simply don't appear.

On higher levels of organization, the mechanisms are equally apparent and even more powerful. The homogeneity of tone I have already remarked upon: a point-blank rifle exchange is described in the same unheightened language, the famed "middle voice" of educated England, as is a tramp through high grass. There is always a clear and fixed point of view, the author's, even—no ventriloquism here—when representations of other outlooks are at issue: "In Anuak fighting among themselves the great object is to take a village from its defenders and destroy it." "It would be quite contrary to Nuer thought, as I have remarked, and it would seem even absurd to them, to say that sky, moon, rain, and so forth are in themselves, singly or collectively, God."[5] There is the suppression of any sign of the struggle with words. Everything that is said is clearly said, confidently and without fuss. Verbally, at any rate, there are no blanks to fill in or dots to join, what you see is what you get, deep reading is not encouraged. And there is the pervasive personal distancing by means of a constant play of the lightest of light irony: nothing really matters enough, not even the Union Jack, for which all this fighting and dying is taking place, to be fully serious about it. Or, more accurately, it is precisely because it does all matter so much that one must not be fully serious about it. Even the strange is more interesting and amusing than it is disturbing or threatening. It bends our categories, but it does not break them.

《》

It is this, so it seems to me, that E-P's text-building strategy—shall we call it "Akobo Realism"?—and the delicate tactics that relentlessly subserve it are all about. The point, the overriding point of every image, every elegance, every nod, is to demonstrate that nothing, no matter how singular, resists reasoned description.

"[The] history of social anthropology," E-P writes toward the beginning of his lecture for the BBC, "Fieldwork and the Empirical Tradition," perhaps the most explicit statement of his view of his vocation, "may be regarded as the substitution, by slow gradations, of informed opinion about primitive peoples for uninformed opinion, and the stage reached in this process at any time is roughly relative to

[5]*Nuer Religion*, p. 2.

the amount of organized knowledge available."[6] The informing of informed opinion (those discerning readers,
with whom that as-you-will-see contract is in force) in the
matter of primitives, as others inform it about Homer, Italian painting, or the English civil war, is anthropology's appointed task; and though it is an extraordinarily difficult
one, it is only practically so.

There are language barriers to be crossed: "Many primitive languages are almost unbelievably difficult to learn" (p.
79). Taxing conditions of work must be endured: "[The] anthropologist is all alone, cut off from the companionship of
men of his own race and culture, and is dependent on the natives around him for company, friendship, and human understanding" (p. 79). And personal biases are not wholly er-
adicable: "One can only interpret what one sees in terms of
one's own experience and of what one is" (p. 84). But the
barriers can be crossed: "[When] one has fully understood
the meaning of all the words of [the natives'] language in all
their situations of reference one has finished one's study of
the society" (p. 80). The conditions can be transcended:
"Anthropological fieldwork . . . requires a certain kind of
character and temperament. . . . To succeed in [it] a man
must be able to abandon himself [to native life] without re-
serve" (pp. 81–82). The biases can be neutralized: "If allow-
ances are made for the personality of the writer, and if we
consider that in the entire range of anthropological studies
the effects of these personal differences tend to correct each
other, I do not think that we need worry unduly over this
problem in so far as the reliability of anthropological findings is in question" (p. 84). We need not, indeed, worry unduly much about anything, except sticking manfully to it:

[6]E. E. Evans-Pritchard, *Social Anthropology* (London, 1957), p. 65.

"It is almost impossible for a person who knows what he is looking for and how to look for it, to be mistaken about the facts if he spends two years among a small and culturally homogeneous people doing nothing else but studying their way of life" (p. 83).

Transferred to the ethnographic page this attitude leads to a string of clean, well-lighted judgments, unconditional statements so perspicuously presented that only the invincibly uninformable will think to resist them. One can find this sort of first-strike assertiveness almost everywhere in E-P's work. In *The Sanusi of Cyrenaica*: "The Bedouin certainly have a profound faith in God and trust in the destiny He has prepared for them." In *The Nuer*: "In a strict sense, the Nuer have no law." In *Witchcraft, Oracles, and Magic Among the Azande*: "Azande undoubtedly perceive a difference between what we consider the workings of nature on the one hand and the workings of magic and ghosts and witchcraft on the other hand." In *Nuer Religion*: "Certainly one cannot speak of any specifically religious emotion among the Nuer." In *Kinship and Marriage Among the Nuer*: "With rare exceptions, I found Nuer women well content with their station and that their husbands and other men treated them with respect."[7]

The question here is not the truth of such statements (though I have my doubts about those Bedouins and those women), nor does Evans-Pritchard fail to support them with extensive and detailed evidence, carefully weighed. They are not *obiter dicta*, however much they may sound like them when torn from context. The question is how does a constant rain of such promulgatory declarations (for one en-

---

[7] E. E. Evans-Pritchard, *The Sanusi of Cyrenaica* (New York, 1949), p. 63; *The Nuer* (Oxford, 1940), p. 162; *Witchcraft*, p. 81; *Nuer Religion*, p. 312; *Kinship and Marriage Among the Nuer* (Oxford, 1951), p. 134.

counters, literally, a half-dozen a half-page) produce (as, particulars aside, it clearly does) a believable account of Libyans or Nilotes or, in other hands, perhaps not quite as sure, Australians, Polynesians, Burmans, or East Africans. How (why? in what way? of what?) does all this resolute informing inform?

Let me first answer this compound question, rather in the E-P manner, with a pair of flat, unshaded assertions— one concerning how he does it, the other concerning what he does—and then, rather in my manner, unflatten these assertions, and shade them, in terms of tendential references to his work. *How he does it*: The outstanding characteristic of E-P's approach to ethnographic exposition and the main source of his persuasive power is his enormous capacity to construct visualizable representations of cultural phenomena—anthropological transparencies. *What he does*: The main effect, and the main intent, of this magic lantern ethnography is to demonstrate that the established frames of social perception, those upon which we ourselves instinctively rely, are fully adequate to whatever oddities the transparencies may turn out to picture.

《》

Though it has not, so far as I can discover, been explicitly commented upon, and certainly never analyzed, the intensely visual quality of Evans-Pritchard's style is so apparent to anyone who has read much of him that a few allusions to particular images is sufficient to call up entire books of his.

There is, the most famous of all, the collapsing granary scene from *Witchcraft, Oracles, and Magic*—those hapless Zande forever taking refuge from the sun under a storehouse precisely at the point at which termites have finally

eaten their way through its supports—fixing in our minds
the whole colliding-causes-and-unfortunate-events theory
of witchcraft E-P develops there.[8] There are the ox-and-
cucumber and the twins-and-birds ideograms from *Nuer
Religion* that virtually every writer on sacrifice or totemism
or "primitive thought" seems obliged to conjure with.
There are the endless cattle celebrations, the flooding grass-
lands with homesteads perched on mounds or strung along
sand ridges, and the "tall, long-limbed, and narrow headed"
spear wavers "strut[ting] about like lords of the earth,
which, indeed, they consider themselves to be" of *The Nuer*
that makes theirs perhaps the most seeable society in the
whole of ethnography.[9] Leopard-skin chiefs, rubbing
boards, dance duels, beehive cattle byres, like the hip shooting, fired huts, and paraded flags with the Anuak: they all
flip by, driving the argument home.

And again, E-P is himself quite conscious of all this, as
aware as we are (or would be if we paid more attention to
such matters than we usually do) that his natural idiom is,
so to speak, optical, his "being there" signature passionately
visual:

When I think of the sacrifices I have witnessed in Nuerland there
are two objects I see most vividly and which sum up for me the sacrificial rite: the spear brandished in the right hand of the officiant
as he walks up and down past the victim delivering his invocation,
and the beast awaiting its death. It is not the figure of the officiant
or what he says which evokes the most vivid impression, but the
brandished spear in his right hand.[10]

Even when it is not a question of direct experience, as in his
account, based on informant memories, in "Zande Kings

8 *Witchcraft*, pp. 70–71.
9 *The Nuer*, pp. 3, 182.
10 *Nuer Religion*, p. 231.

and Princes" of a nineteenth-century king, the language remains intensely visual:

Gubudwe was a short man, though not excessively short. . . . [He] was stout also, not however, unpleasantly stout. He was stout with the stoutness of a man whose flesh is loose with it. His breasts protruded like those of a woman, but not altogether like a woman's for they were a man's breasts. His wrists were wrinkled with fat, and his forearm was like a man's shank. His eyes were little protruding eyes and they sparkled like stars. When he looked at a man in anger they were terrible; then they went grey like ashes.[11]

And this penchant, not to call it something stronger than that, for a see-er's rhetoric is hardly confined, as anyone who looks into his works will be immediately aware, to his verbal text. There are, in the first place, those astonishing photographs, which though they may seem initially to be your standard note-the-clan-marks ethnographic snapshots—"initiation ceremony," "natives fishing," and so on—are, with few exceptions, not so much illustrative as emblematical. Frankly, even ostentatiously posed, so that they seem almost like still lifes, objects arranged for ruminant viewing (a tall, naked cowherd leaning, negligently, legs crossed, against the tension of a tether; a similarly negligent, similarly naked, standing girl, sucking on an elaborate pipe; a seated blind man, hands folded, cradling his spear between his elbow and his neck), or when that is not possible, meticulously composed (tensed warriors flashing spears at a wedding dance; massive cattle, clustering in a downpour; a boy, arms raised like great curving horns, singing praise songs to his ox), the photographs stand irregularly among the word paintings, unreferred to, barely captioned ("Youth," "Au-

[11]E. E. Evans-Pritchard, "Zande Kings and Princes," in E. E. Evans-Pritchard, *Essays in Social Anthropology* (London, 1962), p. 215.

66

gust Shower," "A Maiden, Smoking Pipe"), and for the most part singly, making points of their own.

There are, too, the line drawings. Evans-Pritchard is one of the few modern ethnographers (quite possibly the only one) who seems to have grasped the fact that the photograph has not only not rendered the sketch obsolete, but, as the film has for the photograph, has pointed up its comparative advantage. His books are set off by (again) self-standing, unexplicated sketches ("Cupping Horn," "Neck Rests," "Instrument Used in Wedding Invocations"), rimming, like visual footnotes, the edges of the text. (There are very few verbal footnotes and, notoriously, virtually no professional citations at all. "The literature" is another thing one is expected already to know.)

And there is, finally, the diagramming; the representation—especially in *The Nuer*, that anthropological geometry book—of social structure in terms of a set of elementary plane figures: squares, rectangles, triangles, trees, circles, arcs, rays, matrixes, plus of course the more standard kin charts, graphs, and sketch maps, which also take on, in his hands, a Euclidean look. The blurred edges of social things—villages, tribes, seasons, cattle claims, war, bad magic and good—are drawn onto the page as straight lines and angular shapes, firmly bounded, thoroughly definite. As Ivan Karp and Kent Maynard have pointed out, the argument of *The Nuer*—essentially that society is an enmeshment of relational systems—is importantly held together by the repetition of a single figure, an equilateral triangle, first as a representation of the space-time system, then of the lineage system, and finally of the political system.[12] A similar

12I. Karp and K. Maynard, "Reading *The Nuer*," *Current Anthropology*, 24 (1983): 481–92.

point could be made about the subsectioned (and sub-sub-sectioned) rectangle, which is used to represent tribal organization, intertribal relations, and the feud.

The vignette, the photograph, the sketch, the diagram—these are the organizing forces of E-P's ethnography, which moves by means of decisively imaged ideas, which coheres more as a landscape coheres than as a myth does (or a diary), and which is dedicated, above all things, to making the puzzling plain. His world is a noonday world in which sharply outlined figures, most of them more than a little singular, act in describable ways against perceptible backgrounds. If he is "the Stendhal of anthropology," as Mary Douglas suggests, in a book that otherwise takes a rather different view of him than mine (she thinks of him as a kind of homemade social psychologist), it is not because of his "penetrating" sense of "the delicate strain and balance between desires."[13] (I do not see that he had such a sense.) It is because, like la Sanseverina, his Anuak, Zande, Nuer, Dinka, Shilluk, and Bedouin—and in his texts he himself—subsist.

《》

All this drastic clarity—luminous, dazzling, stunning, . . . blinding—is, to drop the other shoe of my argument, not just an adjunct of Evans-Pritchard's ethnography, not a stylistic quirk or a bit of rhetorical decor laid on to make the facts less wearying; it is the very heart of it. Here, as in *Tristes Tropiques*, the way of saying is the what of saying. But here, in contrast to *Tristes Tropiques*, the what of saying is not that the "tribal," "primitive," "savage," . . . whatever . . . is a world of equatorial shadows and jungle darknesses, the opaque other unreachable behind mirrored glass at the

[13]M. Douglas, *Edward Evans-Pritchard* (New York, 1980), p. 135.

68

end of the Quest. It is one of manifest vitality, distinct and immediate: recognizable, strangely reminiscent, familiar even, if but steadily enough looked at.

As Ernest Gellner has remarked, the abiding concerns of E-P's work, the puzzles to which he again and again returns—the maintenance of cognitive order in the absence of science, the maintenance of political order in the absence of the state, and (though Gellner doesn't mention it) the maintenance of spiritual order in the absence of a church—are aspects of a single concern: how what we take to be the foundations of genuinely human life manages to exist without the assistance of our institutions.[14] E-P's classic studies all begin with the discovery that something we have in our culture is lacking in that of the other: among the Zande, it is our distinction between natural and moral causation; among the Nuer, our structure of state-enforced law and management of violence; in *Nuer Religion*, our "dogma, liturgy, . . . sacrament, . . . cult and mythology" (p. v). And they all end with the discovery that something else—witchcraft, segmentary organization, or a modalistic image of divinity—works well enough instead.

It is this, finally, that Evans-Pritchard's text-building strategy, "Akobo Realism," accomplishes, or anyway seeks to accomplish. It seeks the disenstrangement of apparently bizarre—irrational, anarchic, heathenish—ideas, feelings, practices, values, and so on, not by setting fanciful cultural representations of them out in formal universal orderings but by talking about them in the same equanimous "of course" tone in which one talks, if one is who one is, about one's own values, practices, feelings, and the like. Powerful for "including out," it is, in its tone and in the assumptions

[14]E. Gellner, "Introduction," in E. E. Evans-Pritchard, *A History of Anthropological Thought* (New York, 1981), pp. xiv–xv.

and judgments it projects, equally powerful for including in, and indeed for doing both at the same time. In E-P's hands, that is precisely what this strategy does for his various sorts of Nilotes. Depicting them as not other but otherwise (sensible enough when you get to know them, but with their own way of doing things) causes them to appear to differ from ourselves only in things that do not really matter—"dreadful nuisance[s] most of the time but . . . good to have around in a fight."

The marvel of this rather dialectical approach to ethnography is that it validates the ethnographer's form of life at the same time as it justifies those of his subjects—and that it does the one by doing the other. The adequacy of the cultural categories of, in this case, university England, to provide a frame of intelligible reasonings, creditable values, and familiar motivations for such oddities as poison oracles, ghost marriages, blood feuds, and cucumber sacrifices recommends those categories as of somehow more than parochial importance. Whatever personal reasons E-P may have had for being so extraordinarily anxious to picture Africa as a logical and prudential place—orderly, straightforward and levelheaded, firmly modeled and open to view—in doing so he constructed a forceful argument for the general authority of a certain conception of life. If it could undarken Africa, it could undarken anything.

This bringing of Africans into a world conceived in deeply English terms, and confirming thereby the dominion of those terms, must, however, not be misunderstood. It is not ethnocentricity, except in the trivial sense that all views must be someone's views and all voices come from somewhere. In contrast to what has sometimes been said of him, E-P did not make "his" Anuak, Nuer, *et al.* into black Englishmen; they exist as fully realized as any peoples in the ethnographic literature, their own weight in their own space. Nor is it "they are just like us" that E-P is telling his appointed audience waiting respectfully for informed instruction. Rather, it is that their differences from us, however dramatic, do not, finally, count for much. On the Akobo as on the Isis, men and women are brave and cowardly, kind and cruel, reasonable and foolish, loyal and perfidious, intelligent and stupid, vivid and boring, believing and indifferent, and better the one than the other.

"The least He that is in England," it has been famously said (though we should want now to add an explicit "She") "has a life to live as the greatest He." The extension of that sentiment beyond England to Africa, and farther (perhaps even to Italy, though the matter is difficult), is the purpose of Evans-Pritchard's slide show. And whatever this is—presumptuous, romantic, or merely wildly inadequate ("the English Ideology rides again")—it is not smug nor ungenerous nor uncompassionate. Nor, for that matter, is it untrue.

But the question may not be so much what is true as what is doable. The confidence that self-closing discourse gave to Lévi-Strauss and Akobo Realism to Evans-Pritchard seems to many anthropologists less and less available. Not only are they confronted by societies half modern, half traditional; by fieldwork conditions of staggering ethical complexity; by a host of wildly contrasting approaches to description and analysis; and by subjects who can and do speak for themselves. They are also harassed by grave inner uncertainties, amounting almost to a sort of epistemological hypochondria, concerning how one can know that anything one says about other forms of life is as a matter of fact so.

This loss of confidence, and the crisis in ethnographic writing that goes with it, is a contemporary phenomenon and is due to contemporary developments. It is how things stand with us these days. It is not how they stood for Sir Edward Evan Evans-Pritchard.

4

I-WITNESSING

Malinowski's Children

. . . I went to the village; the moonlit night was bright. I felt not too exhausted. In the village I gave Kavakava a bit of tobacco. Then, since there was no dance or assembly, I walked to Oroobo by way of the beach. Marvelous. It was the first time I had seen this vegetation in the moonlight. Too strange and exotic. The exoticism breaks through lightly, through the veil of familiar things. Went into the bush. For a moment I was frightened. Had to compose myself. Tried to look into my own heart. "What is my inner life?" No reason to be satisfied with myself. The work I am doing is a kind of opiate rather than a creative expression. I am not trying to link it to deeper sources. To organize it. Reading novels [instead of working] is simply disastrous. Went to bed and thought about other things in an impure way. . . .

Nothing whatever draws me to ethnographic studies. I went to the village and I surrendered artistically to the impression of a new *Kulturkreis*. On the whole the village struck me rather unfavorably. There is a certain disorganization, the villages are dispersed; the rowdiness and persistence of the people who laugh and stare and lie discouraged me somewhat. I'll have to find my way in all this. . . .

I visited a few huts in the jungle. Came back; started to read

Conrad. Talked with Tiabubu and Sixpence [natives]—momentary excitement. Then I was again overcome by a terrible melancholy, gray like the sky all around the edges of my inner horizon. I tore my eyes from the book and I could hardly believe that here I was among neolithic savages, and that I was sitting here peacefully while terrible things were going on back there [Europe; this is December 1914]. At moments I had an impulse to pray for Mother. Passivity and the feeling that somewhere, far beyond the reach of any possibility of doing something, horrible things are taking place, unbearable. . . .

Went to the village hoping to photograph a few stages of the *bara* dance. I handed out half-sticks of tobacco, then watched a few dances; then took pictures—but results very poor. Not enough light and they would not pose long enough for time exposures. At moments I was furious at them, particularly because after I gave them their portions of tobacco they all went away. On the whole my feelings toward the natives are decidedly tending to "Exterminate the brutes." In many instances I have acted unfairly and stupidly—about the trip to Domara, for example. I should have given 2 and they would have done it. As a result I certainly missed one of my best opportunities. . . .

Did *not* go to village; wrote a few letters, read Machiavelli. Many statements impressed me extraordinarily; moreover, he is very like me in many respects. An Englishman with an entirely European [that is, non-English] mentality and European problems. . . .

Sketches. (a) Whites. 1. Hon R. De Moleyns, nicknamed Dirty Dick—son of a Protestant Irish lord. A thoroughbred, noble figure. Drunk as a sponge, so long as there is any whiskey to be had. After sobering up . . . fairly reserved and cultured with strikingly good manners and very decent. Poorly educated, little intellectual culture. 2. Alf Greenaway [called] "Arupe." From Ramsgate or Margate—working class background—extremely decent and sympathetic boor. It's "bloody" all the time, and he drops his h's and is married to a native woman and feels miserable in respectable company, especially feminine. Has not the slightest wish to leave New Guinea. (b) Colored. Dimdim ([real name] Owani), [a] modern Orestes—killed his own mother when he ran amok. Nervous, impatient—quite intelligent. Life [here] with De Moleyns [is] completely uncivilized. [He is] unshaven, always wearing pajamas, lives in extraordinary filth, in a house without walls . . . and he likes it. [But it is] much better [staying here] than [it was staying] at the [London Missionary Society] House. Better lubrication. Having a crowd of boys to serve you is very pleasant.[1]

This is, of course, a somewhat free-form collage constructed out of that backstage masterpiece of anthropology, our *The Double Helix*, Bronislaw Malinowski's *A Diary in the Strict Sense of the Term*. The *Diary* was written (in Polish, but with English words, phrases, and even whole passages scattered throughout) in New Guinea and the Trobriand Islands in the years 1914–15 and 1917–18 while Malinowski was carrying out what is, all in all, probably the most famous, and certainly the most mythicized, stretch of field work in the history of the discipline: the paradigm journey to the paradigm elsewhere. It was discovered among his papers after his sudden death in 1942, but only translated and published, amid much handwringing as to the propriety of it all, in 1967. "Certain passages," Raymond Firth, Malinowski's student, friend, and follower, remarks in his extremely uneasy introduction to the book (he sounds as

---

[1] B. Malinowski, *A Diary in the Strict Sense of the Term* (New York, 1967), pp. 30–31, 42–43, 53–54, 69, 77–78, 39. I have collapsed paragraphs, run separated sentences together, spelled out abbreviations, glossed native terms, and made a few other cosmetic adjustments to make things read a bit more easily. Though these passages are all excerpted from the opening section of the book, covering the first four months of an eventual four-year chronicle, a similar sample taken from anywhere in the course of the narrative would give the same picture. Like most private journals, especially by the self-obsessed, nothing much moves in the text but time. The publication of the *Diary* has stimulated a number of other reflections on Malinowski as a writer. See, for example, C. Payne, "Malinowski's Style," *Proceedings of the American Philosophical Society*, 125 (1981): 416–40; J. Clifford, "On Ethnographic Self-Fashioning: Conrad and Malinowski," in T. C. Heller et al., eds., *Reconstructing Individualism* (Stanford, Calif., 1986), pp. 140–62; R. J. Thornton, "'Imagine Yourself Set Down,'" *Anthropology Today*, 1 (Oct. 1985): 7–14.

though he desperately wishes he were someplace else doing almost anything else), "may even nowadays offend or shock the reader, and some readers may be impressed . . . by the revelation of elements of brutality, even degradation, which the record shows on occasion. My own reflection on this is to advise anyone who wishes to sneer at passages in this diary to be first equally frank in his own thoughts and writings, and then judge again" (p. xix).

Aside from remarking that it is hardly a matter of elements and occasional passages, I must before anything else say, especially at a time when defacing monuments is widely perceived as a quick way to anthropological celebrity, that such is my reflection too. The *Diary* disturbs, but not because of what it says about Malinowski. Much of that is neo-romantic commonplace, and, like some other famous "confessions," not nearly so revealing as it seems.[2] It disturbs because of what it says about "Being There."

Whether accurately or not, Malinowski has come down to us, partly because of his own insistence on the fact, partly because of the extraordinary evocativeness of his work, as the prime apostle of what might be called, transforming his own irony, join-the-brutes ethnography. "It is good for the ethnographer," he writes in the famous how-to-do-it introduction to *Argonauts of the Western Pacific*, "to put aside camera, notebook and pencil, and join in himself in what is going on. . . . I am not certain if this is equally easy for everyone—perhaps the Slavonic nature is more plastic and more naturally savage than that of Western Europeans—but though the degree of success varies, the attempt is possible

[2]On the romanticism, see I. Strenski, "Malinowski: Second Positivism, Second Romanticism," *Man*, 17 (1981): 766–70. For my own views as to what the diary "reveals" about Malinowski, see "Under the Mosquito Net," *New York Review of Books*, Sept. 14, 1967.

for everyone." One grasps the exotic not by drawing back from the immediacies of encounter into the symmetries of thought, as with Lévi-Strauss, not by transforming them into figures on an African urn, as with Evans-Pritchard. One grasps it by losing oneself, one's soul maybe, in those immediacies. "Out of such plunges into the life of the natives . . . I have carried away a distinct feeling that . . . their manner of being became more transparent and easily understandable than it had been before."[3]

Like *Tristes Tropiques* and "Operations on the Akobo," *A Diary in the Strict Sense of the Term* (the title is not Malinowski's, but an attempt by the editors to ward off evil spirits) projects us into the peculiarities of a distinct strategy of anthropological text-building with sudden force. As atypical as those other two works, curious and off-schedule, and like them unconventionally written, the *Diary* too resists the settled habits of schoolbench reading.

As my excerpts from it demonstrate, the problem that the *Diary* forefronts, with which—lubrication and Slavonic nature aside—it is almost wholly absorbed, is that there is a lot more than native life to plunge into if one is to attempt this total immersion approach to ethnography. There is the landscape. There is the isolation. There is the local European population. There is the memory of home and what one has left. There is the sense of vocation and where one is going. And, most shakingly, there is the capriciousness of one's passions, the weakness of one's constitution, and the vagrancies of one's thoughts: that nigrescent thing, the self. It is not a question of going native (Alf Greenaway, Ramsgate, working class, can more or less manage that). It is a question of living a multiplex life: sailing at once in several seas.

[3]B. Malinowski, *Argonauts of the Western Pacific* (New York, 1922), pp. 21–22.

Of course, unlike *Tristes Tropiques*, which addresses the world, and anyone else who might be listening, and "Operations on the Akobo," which addresses whoever it is (old boys and historians, I suppose) that reads British army journals, the *Diary* was presumably not written to be published. At least Malinowski seems to have made no move in that direction, though the care with which it is written, and (to the degree one can perceive it through the translation) the vehemence, might well give us pause. As a literary product genre-addressed to an audience of one, a message from the self writing to the self reading, it poses a problem which is nevertheless general, and one that haunts the ethnographic writings of Malinowski (and, as we shall see, not only his) like a spirit-double unreturnable to the bush: how to draw from this cacophony of moonlit nights and exasperating natives, momentary excitements and murderous despairs, an authentic account of an alien way of life. If observing is so personal a business, a pensive stroll on a shadowed beach, is not observation also? When the subject so expands does not the object shrink?

It is, again, essential to see that, despite the vocabulary in which I have just now cast it (and in which, largely because of Malinowski's apotheosis of empathetic field work, it is usually cast), this issue, negotiating the passage from what one has been through "out there" to what one says "back here," is not psychological in character. It is literary. It arises for anyone who adopts what one may call, in a serious pun, the I-witnessing approach to the construction of cultural descriptions. And it does so, and in just about the same form, whatever the actual content of the "I" may be— Cracow-neurasthenic or (to foreshadow a writer I shall be talking about presently) Down-Under upright. To place the reach of your sensibility—rather than, say, that of your analytical powers or of your social code—at the center of your ethnography, is to pose for yourself a distinctive sort of text-building problem: rendering your account credible through rendering your person so. Ethnography takes, obliquely in the 1920's and 1930's, more and more openly today, a rather introspective turn. To be a convincing "I-witness," one must, so it seems, first become a convincing "I."

Malinowski's main way of going about this formidable task was to project in his ethnographical writings two radically antithetical images of what he variously refers to (though, like the morning star, the evening star, and Venus, they all denote the same resplendent object) as "the competent and experienced ethnographer," "the modern anthropological explorer," the fully professional "specialized fieldworker," and the "chronicler and spokesman of . . . a few thousand 'savages,' practically naked."[4] On the one side, there is the Absolute Cosmopolite, a figure of such enlarged capacities for adaptability and fellow feeling, for insinuating himself into practically any situation, as to be able to see as savages see, think as savages think, speak as savages speak, and on occasion even feel as they feel and believe as they believe. On the other, there is the Complete Investigator, a figure so rigorously objective, dispassionate, thorough, exact, and disciplined, so dedicated to wintry truth as to make Laplace look self-indulgent. High Romance and High Science, seizing immediacy with the zeal of a poet and abstracting from it with the zeal of an anatomist, uneasily yoked.

The degree to which Malinowski outside of his texts

[4]B. Malinowski, *Crime and Custom in Savage Society* (London, 1926), p. ix; *The Sexual Life of Savages in Northwestern Melanesia* (New York, 1929), p. xiv; *Argonauts*, p. 18; *Coral Gardens and Their Magic*, 2 vols. (New York, 1935), vol. 1, p. xx.

was, in fact, the one of these or the other is debatable. Marett, his fellow Oceanist, thought him a man who could find his way into the heart of the shyest savage. Frazer, his mentor, held him a quintessential man of science, as did that other rationalist worthy Havelock Ellis. Firth remarks that it is his, Firth's, impression from talking to him that in the field Malinowski's "participation was almost always secondary to his observation." Audrey Richards, like Firth, a pupil, friend, and follower, says that Malinowski "achieved a great measure of personal identification with the people he lived with." Evans-Pritchard, an early pupil also, but perhaps his bitterest personal and professional enemy, says that "he came to know the Trobrianders well," but, out of an "effort to give the appearance of being natural-scientific," produced books about them which are a "morass of verbiage and triviality."[5] Perhaps, even with the *Diary*—from which, like any contradiction, all conclusions can be drawn—it is indeterminable. But that inside his texts (upon which, I suspect, most of these supposedly personal judgments are in fact based) he was *both*—insistently, confusedly, oddly nervously, as though unsure he would be accepted as either—is perhaps the one thing that is clear about him.

In *Coral Gardens*:

In this book we are going to meet the essential Trobriander. Whatever he might appear to others, to himself he is first and foremost a gardener. His passion for his soil is that of a real peasant. He experiences a mysterious joy in delving into the earth, in turning it up, planting the seed, watching the plant grow, mature, and yield the desired harvest. If you want to know him, you must meet him

[5]Firth in S. Silverman, ed., *Totems and Teachers* (New York, 1981), p. 124. Richards in R. Firth, ed., *Man and Culture: An Evaluation of the Work of Bronislaw Malinowski* (London, 1957), pp. 17–18. E. E. Evans-Pritchard, *A History of Anthropological Thought* (New York, 1981), p. 199.

in his yam garden, among his palm groves or on his taro fields. You must see him digging his black or brown soil among the white outcrops of dead coral and building the fence, which surrounds his garden with a "magical wall," which at first gleams like gold among the green of the new growth and then shows bronzed or grey under the rich garlands of yam foliage. (p. xix)

In "Baloma":

In the field one has to face a chaos of facts, some of which are so small that they seem insignificant; others loom so large that they are hard to encompass with one synthetic glance. But in this crude form they are not scientific facts at all; they are absolutely elusive, and can be fixed only by interpretation, by seeing them *sub specie aeternitatis*, by grasping what is essential in them and fixing this. *Only laws and generalizations are scientific facts*, and field work consists only and exclusively in the interpretation of the chaotic social reality, in subordinating it to general rules.[6]

In *The Sexual Life of Savages*:

The reader will find that the natives treat sex in the long run not only as a source of pleasure, but, indeed, as a thing serious and even sacred. Nor do their customs and ideas eliminate from sex its power to transform crude material fact into wonderful spiritual experience, to throw the romantic glamour of love over the technicalities of love making. . . . It is perhaps in the blending of the directly sensual with the romantic and in the wide and weighty sociological consequences of what to start with is the most personal event—it is in this richness and multiplicity of love that lies its philosophic mystery, its charm for the poet and its interest for the anthropologist. (p. xxiv)

In *Argonauts*:

The results of scientific research in any branch of learning ought to be presented in a manner absolutely candid and above board. No one would dream of making an experimental contribution to

---

[6]B. Malinowski, "Baloma," in B. Malinowski, *Magic, Science and Religion, and Other Essays* (Boston, 1948), p. 238 (first published, 1916). Italics in original.

physical or chemical science, without giving a detailed account of all the arrangements of the experiments; an exact description of the apparatus used; of the manner in which the observations were conducted; of their number; of the length of time devoted to them, and of the degree of approximation with which each such measurement was made. . . . I consider that only such ethnographic sources are of unquestionable scientific value, in which we can clearly draw the line between, on the one hand, the results of direct observation and of native statements and interpretations, and on the other, the inferences of the author. (pp. 2–3)

And so it goes. This oscillation between what I earlier called the anthropologist as pilgrim and as cartographer appears and reappears, like a rhetorical tic, throughout the whole of the more than twenty-five hundred pages of descriptive work (much of it, I should say, so as not to be seen as antiempirical, superb) that Malinowski produced on the Trobriands. Indeed, in most such this-is-your-author-speaking passages, the two identities advance and recede almost from line to line, to the point where one comes to feel he is faced with a strange sort of sincere forger trying desperately to copy his own signature.

Again, it is not that Malinowski doesn't know who, "inside," he really is or who, "outside," he wants to present himself as being: he is, if anything, too sure of both. It is that, more than any ethnographer before him and most after him, he is constantly aware, and makes us constantly aware, of just how difficult the passage is, and how uncharted, from knocking about with the essential savage amid the vines and corals of a ragged yam garden to engraving a measured and law-governed social reality in *aeternitatis* paragraphs. "In Ethnography," he writes in the *Argonauts*, capitalizing "Ethnography" as (like "Ethnographer") he almost always does, "the distance is . . . enormous between the brute material . . . as it is presented . . . in the kaleidoscope of tribal life . . . and the final authoritative presentation of the results" (pp. 3–4). That perception, one not about field technique, not about social theory, not even about that sainted object, "social reality," but about "the discourse problem" in anthropology—how to author an authoritative presentation—may be his most consequential legacy. Certainly it has turned out to be his most besetting one.

For, long before the *Diary* was available to dramatize the fact for the inattentive, Malinowski posed the "Being There" question in its most radical, if not necessarily its most productive, form. He projected at once (never mind how fully he practiced it) a mode of research that, at its limits anyway, virtually erases, or claims to, the affective distance between the observer and the observed, and a style of analysis (never mind how consistently he pursued it) that, at its limits, renders that distance, or pretends to, near absolute. The tension between what are, in the end, the archetypal moments in ethnographical experience, soaking it up and writing it down, was thus raised to an extraordinary pitch. In Malinowski's works, this tension was more or less held at bay, and in fact put to rhetorical use, by the persistent equivocation, now bottomless mysteries, now triumphant laws, to which I have been pointing. But for those later ethnographers, perhaps by now a majority of those under 40, in whom Malinowski's field work ideals remain very much alive, more alive in some ways than they were in him, but for whom his analytical ones are not just dead but despised, the matter has not been so simple. They have been willed not, as so often thought, a research method, "Participant Observation" (that turns out to be a wish not a method), but a literary dilemma, "Participant Description."

《》

The problem, to rephrase it in as prosaic terms as I can manage, is to represent the research process in the research product; to write ethnography in such a way as to bring one's interpretations of some society, culture, way of life, or whatever and one's encounters with some of its members, carriers, representatives, or whomever into an intelligible relationship. Or, quickly to refigure it again, before psychologism can set in, it is how to get an I-witnessing author into a they-picturing story. To commit oneself to an essentially biographical conception of Being There, rather than a reflective, an adventural, or an observational one, is to commit oneself to a confessional approach to text-building. The real-world persona that Lévi-Strauss, Evans-Pritchard, and Malinowski sought to confine to their fables, their memoirs, or their reveries, that creatural self that has essayed odd things and suffered odder ones, now floods out into the work itself.

The most direct way to bring field work as personal encounter and ethnography as reliable account together is to make the diary form, which Malinowski used to sequester his impure thoughts in scribbled Polish, into an ordered and public genre—something for the world to read. This is essentially what Kenneth Read, whose 1965 book, *The High Valley*, is one of the first, and one of the best, attempts to construct I-witness style ethnography, has done.

Read, an Australian anthropologist, trained there and in Britain under first-generation Malinowski students, and until his retirement a few years ago a professor at the University of Washington in Seattle, worked in the same part of the world as Malinowski (though on mainland New Guinea rather than its offshore islands, and just after the Second World War rather than in the middle of the First). And, like Malinowski, he has a get-it-all-in approach to ethnography and a let-it-all-out approach to prose. But in just about every other way the two men, at least as they emerge in the elaborate self-fashionings of their books, could hardly be more different. Instead of Dostoevskian darkness and Conradian blur, the Readian "I" is filled with confidence, rectitude, tolerance, patience, good nature, energy, enthusiasm, optimism—with an almost palpable determination to do what is right and think what is proper. If the *Diary* presents the image of a womanizing cafe intellectual cast among savages, *The High Valley* presents one of an indefinite country vicar.

"Why, then," Read asks on the first page of his preface, in what has since become the standard first move in this sort of close-up anthropology, its key signature,

Why, then, is so much anthropological writing so antiseptic, so devoid of anything that brings a people to life? There they are, pinned like butterflies in a glass case, with the difference, however, that we often cannot tell what color these specimens are; and we are never shown them in flight, never see them soar or die except in generalities.

The field-working anthropologist undergoes a unique experience; no one else knows quite so personally what it is like to live in an entirely alien culture. Missionaries do not know; government officials do not know; traders and explorers do not know. Only the anthropologist wants nothing from the people with whom he lives— nothing, that is, but . . . an understanding of and an appreciation for the texture of their lives.[7]

This last bit of guild self-congratulation aside (one would think he might have at least admitted that we want publications), Read does seem to have approached his Papuans with an unusual openness and generosity of spirit, and to have been, as is only just, rewarded for it. "Looking back

[7]K. E. Read, *The High Valley* (New York, 1965), p. ix; I have reversed the order of these passages.

now," he writes, "I believe I was permanently elated. At least this is the only name I can give to a state of mind in which certainty in my own abilities and discovery of myself joined with a compassion for others and a gratitude for the lessons in acceptance that they taught me" (p. 7). This is strong stuff for "us moderns" to swallow. As Tocqueville remarks somewhere, the one thing we are not allowed to do any more is speak well of ourselves, and Malinowski's "what an unconscionable wretch I am" seems somehow the authentic voice of candor. But by the time Read closes his book, embracing, unembarrassed at last, his main informant in one of those astonishing all-over Papuan bear-hugs (as they are likely to grab hold of your genitals, you can hardly be more "there" than that) and hoping "that he [the informant] felt . . . in the pressure of my hands, the only gift I have, the only one I need to receive" (p. 318), all but diehard apostles of the hermeneutics of suspicion should be at least somewhat brought round, whatever they may suppose about the nature of the gift.

The bulk of Read's book consists, then, of a series of brilliantly realized, if somewhat overwrought set pieces, all opalescent mists and flickering brown eyes, in which his reserved, rather introversive temperament is passed, like so many spiritual tests, through various Papuan actualities: the brutal and blood-drenched initiation of a dreamy young houseboy of his; the compelled marriage of a frightened young neighbor girl, sent abruptly from childhood to be a woman elsewhere; the unjust imprisonment by the Colonial Administration (Australian, of course) of a quarrelsome, but fascinating and in his own way admirable, malcontent. "[My] desire to experience the quality of primitive life," he says, " . . . had become a personal need that was quite as important to me as any contribution to knowledge coming from my work" (p. 20). We are faced, indeed, with another Quest. But this one is less for noesis and the fathomable Other, than for redemption and the acceptable Self. And it does not fail, it succeeds. Or so, fervidly, we are over and over assured.

The means of this assurance is, as I say, the presentation of a set of very heavily written but extremely well-constructed recognition dramas. (Read's is one of those plethoric styles—aiming at Proust, but arriving, usually, rather closer to Lawrence Durrell—that those who like that sort of thing call "poetic" and those who don't call "cloying.") Each such drama, a chapter to itself, entitled with its principal's name—Makis, Asemo, Tarova, Goluwaizo—begins with images of isolation (still viridian pools, motionless hieratic shrubs), proceeds through images of confused perception (babbling voices, fluttering head feathers), to a final epiphany, compact and painful, that informs the soul.

In the houseboy story, which we can take as an example, for they all have the same structure, and indeed the same message—compassion cleanses—the revelatory moment is the male initiation rite, a matter, among other things, of drawing great quantities of blood from the nose by violently invading it with sticks of wadded leaves.

The implications for Asemo [the houseboy] were brought home to me suddenly as the last of the bloodstained figures staggered up the gravel beach. . . . My search for him . . . had brought me within several paces of where he stood. Like his age mates, his arms were held by two men . . . the contrast of their plumes and paint investing his own unadorned nakedness with almost sacrificial innocence. . . . I am sure he did not recognize me. His own eyes saw nothing but the need to marshal the defenses of his body for the imminent act of violation, and he could not have been more unaware of the manner in which my heart rushed toward him. It was not simply the thought of his suffering that closed off my senses so that momentarily we were alone in the shimmer of light and water, facing each other across a void, the noises and smells of the crowd nothing more than a remote intrusion beating unsuccessfully against the boundaries of recognition. Everything I had gradually learned of him in the past few months returned to me, rendered more vivid by the weeks of separation, so that I realized suddenly the gap his precipitate departure had left; and the loss stabbed the more sharply because I saw him, now, clearly projected against a screen of impersonal events whose sweep ignored the justifications for his present predicament. . . .

[At] this moment [Asemo] stood [in my mind] for the inarticulate aspirations of a people thrust unwillingly into the uncharted seas of time, and I was struck suddenly by a feeling of poignant futility, a compound of sympathy for those who acted as though the past still showed a viable perspective on the world ahead, and a deeper pain for those whose visions of a possible future blinded them to the externally imposed limits of reality. This was precisely where Asemo stood. The figure of his [ritual] sponsor concealed him from me as he received the thrust of the purifying leaves, but when the older man moved aside, his violent mission done, the bright blood flowing from Asemo's lowered head was like a hopeless offering for peace between embattled opposites.

My recollection of the day's subsequent events is curiously anticlimactic, though in fact the tension and the violence grew in intensity. . . . But everything of personal importance had been said to me when Asemo's blood reddened the water, and the things he suffered after this seemed like an unnecessary reiteration, an example of the [Papuan's] exhausting tendency to seek excess. (pp. 167–68)

The succession of these transforming moments of inward passion (there are perhaps a dozen in all) thus form the narrative line by which his ethnography is driven. In the end, after two years of such iterating excitements, he falls desperately ill, as one might have predicted, with a bleeding ulcer. The nearest hospital is far away on the coast. Rather than being flown there, he elects to remain in a local medical assistant's house, within sight of his village. Soon the villagers begin to come to his bedside, drawing him back into their world, "their very names echoing with the rhythm of a life that once seemed so alien, but that now fell from my tongue like the movement of my own heart" (p. 318). And when, recovered, he finally leaves, there is that redemptive embrace and a decade later, this is not quite diary, not quite monograph, eluding, so he thinks, the Malinowskian dilemma:

This record has been unequivocally subjective. I have hoped to convey something of the quality of [Papuan] life . . . as it appeared through my own eyes, filtered through my own background, my likes and dislikes, qualified by my own strengths and weaknesses. I believe that my professional training fosters an objectivity that has prevented me from making egregious errors in characterizing the [Papuans], and it has also helped me to see myself . . . more clearly. Yet this is not what I would write if my motivation had been solely the canons of professional scholarship, any more than it is all I would tell if it had been to my purpose to reveal myself entirely. I have tried to steer a middle course between these two extremes. (p. 310)

《》

Perhaps he has. But, as in the case of Malinowski himself, one may wonder whether what Roland Barthes, who should know, has called the "diary disease" is so easily cured, whether working up a private self for public presentation is so readily managed. In a piece mischievously called *Délibération*, Barthes asks himself

[Should] I keep a journal *with a view to publication*? Can I make the journal into a "work"? . . . [The] aims traditionally attributed to the intimate Journal . . . are all connected to the advantages and the prestige of "sincerity" (to express yourself, to explain yourself, to judge yourself); but psychoanalysis, the Sartrean critique of bad faith, and the Marxist critique of ideologies have made "confession" a futility: sincerity is merely second-degree Image-repertoire.[8]

The task of the journal writer—that is, in my terms (at once broader and narrower than Barthes's), anyone who takes a strongly I-witnessing approach to ethnographic text-building—is, as he says in that libidinal way of his, to constitute the author as an object of desire; it is "to seduce, by that swivel which shifts from writer to person . . . to prove that 'I am worth more than what I write'" (p. 481). A sense of the inessential, the uncertain, the inauthentic somehow clings to such writings and, these days, to the writers of such writings: "What a paradox! By choosing the most 'direct,' the most 'spontaneous' forms of writing, I find myself to be the clumsiest of ham actors" (p. 493).

In short: "'I' is harder to write than to read" (p. 487). And if we look around at anthropological writing right now, or at least at the more searching and original of such writing, the signs of this, of the journal-into-work mode of text-building and the literary anxieties that plague it, are to be seen on all sides. The "diary disease" is now endemic. So, in spades, is *délibération*.

How to convey this mood—an enormous tangle of epistemological, moral, ideological, vocational, and personal doubts, each feeding upon the others, and mounting at times to something very near Pyrrhonism—is itself a bit of a problem. A general survey is hardly possible, would not communicate much to a nonprofessional audience, and anyway has already been well carried out, for the professional

---

[8]R. Barthes, "Deliberation," in S. Sontag, ed., *A Barthes Reader* (New York, 1982), pp. 479–95; quote from pp. 480–81, italics in original.

audience, by a number of hands.[9] To take a single case on the model of Read and Malinowski seems inadvisable, because, as we are speaking now of an oncoming generation, the scene is less ordered, relative standing less established. We really don't know yet who the "authors" are, who will discourse in whose discursivity, and indeed who will go on discoursing—discoursing ethnography, anyway—at all.

I would like, therefore, quite briefly, quite arbitrarily, and in a brisk, news-from-the-front sort of way, to consider three recent examples, different among themselves in tone, subject matter, and specific approach (to say nothing, as I shall try to, of quality), yet clearly of the mode: Paul Rabinow's *Reflections on Fieldwork*; Vincent Crapanzano's *Tuhami*; and Kevin Dwyer's *Moroccan Dialogues*.

The trio is useful for a number of reasons in conveying a sense of where "Malinowski's Dilemma," "Participant Description," the "Diary Disease," "I-Witnessing," or whatever we want to call it has now got itself to—perhaps most importantly because they form not just an imaginary group, a rounding up of the usual suspects, but a real one, a true growing-up-together cohort. About the same age, status, and reputation, they not only know one another personally, they have also reacted and continue to react to one another's work, so that each of their books as it has appeared has seemed like a contribution to an ongoing conversation, far from ended and not entirely on stage. All three have worked in Morocco, and two of them have produced, in addition to these I-witness works, more standard sorts of ethnographies. A small world, but a definite one.

---

[9]See, e.g., G. Marcus and D. Cushman, "Ethnographies as Texts," in B. Siegel, ed., *Annual Review of Anthropology*, vol. 11 (Palo Alto, Calif., 1982), pp. 25–69.

Also a compendious one. Although each of these writers is concerned with, in a slogan Rabinow, as the first in the series, borrows from Paul Ricoeur and the others then borrow in turn from him, "the comprehension of the self by the detour of the other,"[10] each of them constructs a different sort of quasi-journal, places a different sort of being-there persona at its center, and arrives at a different sort of sincerity crux at its end. Together, they encompass a good part of what is happening to the inheritors of the Malinowskian ideal of immersionist ethnography.

So far as text-form is concerned, Rabinow's book is organized as a sequence of encounters with informants—a faded French cafe-keeper; a manipulative storekeeper *cum* Arabic teacher; a semi-urban, semi-rural, semi-friendly layabout; a neurasthenic village intellectual—the meaning of each such encounter dependent, as he says, upon the next, and so on to some dispiriting conclusion: a rather classic *éducation sentimentale*. Crapanzano's study, subtitled "Portrait of a Moroccan," consists of an extended, drifting, hyper-interpretive interview of the psychoanalytic type—a knowing question asker and a life-damaged self-revealer, locked together (in this case along with a third party, a nonlocal Moroccan, carefully referred to as an "assistant") away from the distractions of ongoing life, in a clinical closet. And finally, Dwyer's book (*his* subtitle is "Anthropology in Question") is also dialogical in form, though here the interviewing is ethnographic and integrally presented, rather than psychoanalytic and selectively so. The informant is guided through a more or less orthodox set of topics—circumcision, migration, festivals, marriages, quarrels, parties—each prefaced by observations of relevant events outside the in-

[10] See P. Rabinow, *Reflections on Fieldwork* (Berkeley, Calif., 1977), p. 5.

terview situation, the whole followed by an extended attack on other ways of doing anthropology, or indeed doing it at all.

The "I's" these writers then invent—"invent," of course, in the sense of construction, not imposture—to serve as the organizing consciousness of these works, Barthes's ham actors and seducing selves, correspond in turn to the text-form employed. Indeed, they define it.

Rabinow, reminding one again of some Frédéric abroad, is the pal, comrade, companion—*copain*, to stay in the idiom—knocking about here and there, going as the occasion goes, with various manners of men (this being Morocco, women, wantons aside, cannot be reached this way); a rather obliging figure, as much bemused as anything else, carried along in a flux of largely accidental, generally shallow, often enough transient sociability: a curing seance; a roadside quarrel; a country idyll. This image of a tossed-about experiencer begins, in fact, before he comes to Morocco, departing Chicago two days after Robert Kennedy's assassination, and continues after he leaves it again, returning to post-Sixties New York ("The 'revolution' had occurred during my absence"); so that the Moroccan sojourn is represented as an interlude, a chapter of happenings, diffuse and episodic, but for all that edifying, and to be followed by others. There is life after field work: "Writing this book seems to have enabled me . . . to begin again on a different terrain" (pp. 148–49).

But if Rabinow in his pages (I am, of course, speaking of him and his colleagues only as they function *inside* their pages, not as "real persons") is the unfinished man, vague to himself, vague to others, Crapanzano, in his, is very highly defined indeed, a sculpted figure, worked and polished: The

Man of Letters (his own characterization of himself, in fact; though here, too, putting the thing in French, *homme de lettres*, gets the tone of it better—Sartre, not Emerson).[11]

Tuhami, the "illiterate Moroccan tilemaker . . . considered an outsider, an outcast even, by the people around him," who "lived alone in a dark, windowless [urban] hovel," and who regarded himself as married to "a capricious, vindictive she-demon, a camel-footed . . . spirit named 'A'isha Qandisha" (pp. 4–5), tells a rather random story of a rather random life in short-takes—this sickness, that job, pilgrimages, dreams, losses, sexual fantasies. The ethnographer-curer, self-conscious to a fault—"Was I frozen before Tuhami?" (p. 136); "I wanted to possess everything that [he] knew . . . and even more" (p. 134); "Perhaps I did not hear his cry for personal recognition" (p. 114)—connects what he is hearing, chimeras and fragments, to the dizzier heights of modern European culture—Lacan and Freud, Nietzsche and Kierkegaard, d'Annunzio and Simmel, Sartre and Blanchot, Heidegger and Hegel; Genet, Gadamer, Schutz, Dostoevsky, Jung, Frye, Nerval—through long, winding passages of bookish meditation. By the time he is finished, he has compared this feckless day laborer from the Meknes medina to some formidable figures indeed—to Sartre's Genet: "Like . . . Genet, Tuhami deigned 'to take notice of the circumstances of his life only insofar as they seem to repeat the original drama of lost Paradise'" (p. 84); to Dostoevsky's underground man: "Perhaps like the hero or . . . antihero . . . [of Dostoevsky's novel] he derives a benefit . . . from being a victim" (p. 83); and at a particularly giddy point to Nerval: "There are striking parallels between this French romantic . . . and Tuhami. Like Tuhami, Nerval

[11]V. Crapanzano, *Tuhami, Portrait of a Moroccan* (Chicago, 1980), p. 145.

split his women into many refractions—and condensed them into single figures of mysterious ontological status" (p. 130n). He is, our anti-hero, Lacan's *manque à être*, Sartre's "we-subject," Simmel's social individual (pp. 140, 148, 136). If the face of the sitter gets a bit difficult to locate in this high-wrought "portrait," that of the portraitist seems clear enough.

Dwyer's book is, as mentioned, also a one-on-one proposition—a "Self and Other," as he puts it, capitalizing the eternal colloquists in the usual way, "becoming interdependent . . . sometimes challenging, sometimes accommodating one another."[12] But as the aim in this case is to expose the unsolid ground upon which all such interaction inevitably rests, a tissue of careerism, deception, manipulation, and micro-imperialism, the Self, rather than being rhetorically aggrandized is, no less rhetorically, undercut. Dwyer's "I" neither floats through his text nor engulfs it. It apologizes for being there at all.

It is Dwyer's view that just about all of anthropology, including, in a sort of Cretan paradox, his own, is "dishonest . . . pernicious and self-serving"; that it is an extension of the "Western societal project"—imperialist, intrusive and disruptive—to "pose all the questions" and assess all the answers; that the practice of it leads, even "in the best of cases," to "personal despair"; and that its main animus, concealed of course and mystified, is to "[shield] the Self and . . . distance and disarm [and thus dominate] the Other" (pp. xxii, 284, 271, xxii). Even the vanguard, struggling to escape all this, merely gets itself (such is the power of Western Ideology disguised as the Search for Truth) more deeply entan-

---

[12] K. Dwyer, *Moroccan Dialogues: Anthropology in Question* (Baltimore, Md., 1982), p. xviii.

gled in it. Rabinow's "Self and Other are too abstract and too general, and the Self shows a certain disregard for the Other"; Crapanzano's "evocative homage to the Other is . . . a self-fulfilling homage to the Self" (p. 280n). We have met the Unreliable Narrator, to recycle Pogo's famous line, and He is Us.

The question that arises, of course, is how anyone who believes all this can write anything at all, much less go so far as to publish it. Dwyer solves the problem, for himself anyway, by combining a radically factualist approach to the reporting of his "dialogues"—the words, the whole words, and nothing but the words—with a radically introversive approach to his role in them.

His interviews with his Moroccan (a prosperous, 65-year-old farmer, rather better put together than Crapanzano's tilemaker) are, as mentioned, quite standard, rather flattened even, both in form and content. Dwyer asks about one thing or another, and the farmer answers: "Why do you have the children circumcised?" "It's a duty." "What qualities do you look for in a Partner?" "In a partner trust is the most important quality" (pp. 58, 144). It's all, as the farmer, who has apparently been to town a couple of times, neatly puts it when Dwyer requests his permission to "make a book" of their conversations, like a courtroom transcript—exact, complete, and unequally informative (p. ix). And then around the interviews, in preludes before them, reflections after them, and footnotes under them, there is a great collection of second, third, and fourth, Minsk-and-Pinsk thoughts—"Why did I ask that? What am I really doing? What does he really think of me? What does he think I think of him?"

The final result of all this transcript ethnography and

annotative soul-searching is, in any case, the image of an almost unbearably earnest field worker, burdened with a murderously severe conscience, and possessed of a passionate sense of mission. He even appends an earnest "Postscript" defending his earnestness: "Would an irreverent style . . . have been more appropriate?" No—exposing the Self and protecting the Other "is . . . no joke" (p. 287). In Dwyer's "I," *the "I" that he writes*, we have neither an adaptable experience collector trying to catch a glimpse of himself in the reactions of others, nor a *mondain* intellectual, assimilating proletarian miseries to literary categories, but a determined moralist: the last angry man—or, one of Flaubert's "Jesuits of the future," the first.

But what is, to me anyway, finally most interesting about all three of these attempts (and most of the others— they appear almost by the week—I have read) to produce highly "author-saturated," supersaturated even, anthropological texts in which the self the text creates and the self that creates the text are represented as being very near to identical, is the strong note of disquiet that suffuses them. There is very little confidence here and a fair amount of outright malaise. The imagery is not of scientific hope compensating inner weakness, à la Malinowski, or of bear-hug intimacy dispelling self-rejection, à la Read, neither of which is very much believed in. It is of estrangement, hypocrisy, helplessness, domination, disillusion. Being There is not just practically difficult. There is something corrupting about it altogether.

For Rabinow, the name of this something is "Symbolic Violence." Reflecting on his playing of various informants off against one another in order to uncover some village conflicts they don't want uncovered, he writes:

97

My response was essentially an act of violence; it was carried out on a symbolic level, but it was violence nonetheless. I was transgressing the integrity of my informants. . . . I knew [what I was doing] would coerce, almost blackmail, [them] into explaining aspects of their lives which they had thus far passionately shielded from me. . . . To those who claim that some form of symbolic violence was not part of their own field experience, I reply simply that I do not believe them. It is inherent in the structure of the situation. (pp. 129–30)

For Crapanzano it is Eros-Thanatos, as he follows up the line quoted earlier about wanting to possess everything and more that Tuhami knew:

I have always been fascinated by d'Annunzio's portrayal, in *The Triumph of Death* (1900), of hero and heroine's obsessive desire to know each other fully. The presumption that such knowledge can be achieved rests either on the belief in total sexual possession—a possession that ends up, as d'Annunzio understood, in total extinction—or on the reduction of the Other to that which is completely graspable: the specimen. The one, the goal of passion, and the other, the product of science, are not in fact so easily separable. Both are of course illusory. (p. 134)

And for Dwyer, it is Domination:

The contemplative stance [he means "pretense"] . . . pervades anthropology, disguising the confrontation between Self and Other, and rendering the discipline powerless to address the vulnerability of the Self. . . . [It] has confronted the Other in a manner that works to muffle the Other's potential challenge. This adds a regrettable new dimension to the dominance that has enabled the anthropologist to initiate encounters with the Other in the first place: that dominance which consistently challenges the Other, is now buttressed by an epistemology that does not allow the Other to challenge the Self. (p. 269)

These dark views, progressing on to even darker ones, may or may not be implicit in the I-witnessing genre, as

Barthes ("[The] defect is existential") thinks they are.[13] But they certainly tend to be characteristic of works, contemporary works anyway, in which representations of the ethnographer's field research conceived as personal experience, "a comprehension of the self by the detour of the other," are placed at the author-izing center. "I" is indeed very hard to write; "I am worth more than what I write," very hard to prove; "second-degree Image-repertoire," very hard to avoid. The sincerity crux awaits all who pass this way. For some, the result of coming to see this is a movement away from ethnography toward metascientific reflection, cultural journalism, or social activism. And for others, resolute and less easily dismayed, and upon whom a great deal depends, it is a redoubled effort to meet the literary challenges left by the Malinowskian legacy. "I-witnessing" may not be altogether well; but it is very much alive.

There is, for example, now a book of Kenneth Read's, published since this essay was originally written, describing two brief summer trips he made to his New Guinea site in 1981 and 1982 after an absence of nearly thirty years: *Return to the High Valley: Coming Full Circle.*[14] Much more flatly written than the earlier book (the lyricism returns only when, intermittently, he recalls scenes from the original stay or quotes from *The High Valley*), and cast in something of a where-are-the-warriors-of-yesteryear idiom, it has a curiously half-hearted, well-if-I-must-I-must quality: as though he knew that it really was a dubious idea to go back and a worse one to write about it.

The town now has paved streets, public water and elec-

[13]Barthes, "Deliberation," p. 494.
[14]K. E. Read, *Return to the High Valley: Coming Full Circle* (Berkeley, Calif., 1986).

tricity, a hotel, and a tavern; public drunkenness is wide-spread; dress is mostly Western; and his closest friend, he of the great bear-hug— "[His] presence breathes in everything I wrote. . . . My relationship with him was as complex as those we have with anyone we love, yet it was as strong as any, despite the greater impediments of the worlds of differences separating us" (p. 252)—is dead, killed a dozen years earlier in a stupid drunken accident, hit by a truck while staggering home from the hotel bar. In the village the houses are milled board rectangles with galvanized iron roofs, the major rituals are no longer performed, Christian Fundamentalism has set in, and the place is full of groaning trucks and cars. "Money is important now. . . . The cries of the flutes are no longer heard in Asemo valley. . . . The landscape [has] an emptiness it did not have when [youths, now in school all day] used to appear suddenly from among the grasses [with their] long headdresses . . ." (pp. 45, 184, 248–49).

Read, as always right-minded, and anxious not to be seen as an old man mired in the past, struggles against the depression all this naturally induces in him: the position of women is far better now; the youth have found new recreations in dusk-to-dawn disco dancing and B-movie going; there is much more contact among different groups and much more traveling outside the area; some of the natives are richer than he is. But it is all rather *voulu*, convincing neither him nor us. "I did not feel [reluctant] about leaving this time. Indeed, it was almost a relief to know there were only two days left" (p. 246).

The book is a postscript, both to a work and to a life, or as he himself suggests (weakly denying that it is so), a series of footnotes revising away what he had written about the

Fifties "until there [is] nothing left but a faint trace of ambience" (p. 22). For all that, however, and in part because of it, the book is, in its own pale way, as moving, if not so passionate, so inward, or so finely wrought as *The High Valley*.[15]

[15] For some other recent examples of I-witnessing ethnographies that are less disconsolate than those of Rabinow, Crapanzano, and Dwyer, and yet connect the confessional side of the genre more firmly to the ethnographic side, see J.-P. Dumont, *The Headman and I: Ambiguity and Ambivalence in the Fieldworking Experience* (Austin, Tex., 1978); E. V. Daniel, *Fluid Signs* (Berkeley, Calif., 1984); and B. Meyerhoff, *Number Our Days* (New York, 1978). In Dumont, the high farce of a perpetually awkward French academic stumbling about among Venezuelan blow-pipe Indians is made to reveal aspects of the latter's life that standard ethnographic descriptive devices could not reach. In Daniel, the indeterminacies of a "native Tamil speaker, born in the Sinhalese speaking south of Sri Lanka to a South Indian Tamil father who changed his name from something divine to something daring in order to marry my mother, a Sri Lankan Anglican whose mother tongue was English" (p. 57) studying his own culture bring out the deeper indeterminacies of the culture itself. In Meyerhoff, the encounter of a young, assimilated, Jewish "lady professor" and a community of aged, traditionalistic, diaspora Jews living out the remains of their lives in a Southern California beach community yields an urgent account of a cultural end game.

5

US / NOT-US

Benedict's Travels

"The Uses of Cannibalism"

We have done scant justice to the reasonableness of cannibalism. There are in fact so many and such excellent motives possible to it that mankind has never been able to fit all of them into one universal scheme, and has accordingly contrived various diverse and contradictory systems the better to display its virtues.

The present decade, indeed, is likely to appreciate to an unusual degree the advantages that attach to cannibalism so soon as the matter may be presented. We have already had recourse to many quaint primitive customs our fathers believed outmoded by the progress of mankind. We have watched the dependence of great nations upon the old device of the pogrom. We have seen the rise of demagogues, and even in those countries we consider lost in a morally dangerous idealism we have watched death dealt out to those who harbor the mildest private opinions. Even in our own country we have come to the point of shooting in the back that familiar harmless annoyance, the strike picketer. It is strange that we have overlooked cannibalism.

Mankind has for many thousands of years conducted experiments in the eating of human flesh, and has not found it wanting. Especially it has been proved to foster the feeling of solidarity within the group and of antipathy toward the alien, providing an incomparable means of gratifying with deep emotion the hatred of one's enemy. Indeed, all the noblest emotions have been found not only compatible with it, but reinforced by its practice. It would appear that we have rediscovered that specific and sovereign remedy for which we have long perceived statesmen to be groping. . . .

It is necessary first to place beyond doubt the high moral sentiments with which the custom has been allied. It has been unfortunate that in our solicitude lest heroism, endurance, and self-control should perish from a world so largely devoted to commerce and the pursuit of wealth, we should have overlooked the matter of cannibalism. Certain valiant tribes of the Great Lakes and the prairies long ago made use of it to this purpose. It was to them their supreme gesture of homage to human excellence. It is told by old travelers that of three enemies whose death made the occasion for such a celebration of their valor, two were eaten with honor, while the one remaining was passed over untouched. For at death, this one had marked himself a coward, and cried out under torture. . . .

This is of course not the only excellent ethical use to which cannibalism has been put among the peoples of the world. There are tribes to whom it is an expression of tenderness to the most nearly related dead so as to dispose of their discarded bodies—a supreme cherishing of those for whom there can be no other remaining act of tenderness. . . .

Cannibalism has proved also to be extraordinarily well qualified to provide the excitement of an ultimate aggression. This has proved recently to be by no means the frivolous subject that it may appear. Indeed we have been confronted by the problem on such a large scale that, in the interests of progress, it is difficult not to press the matter. Without the infantile ostentations and unfortunate appeals to the hatred of one's fellow being which characterize our Black Shirts and our Red Shirts, the Indians of Vancouver Island found a heightened excitation, disciplined in endless ritual and taboo, in a ceremonial show of cannibalism. . . . When it was time for [an aristocrat] to become a member of [a secret] society, he retired to the forests or the graveyard, and it was said that the spirits had taken him. Here an almost mummified corpse was prepared and smoked, and at the appointed time, in the midst of great excitement, the noble youth returned to the village with the Spirit of the Cannibal upon him. A member of the society carried the corpse before him, while with violent rhythms and trembling of his tense body, he rendered in dance his seeking for human flesh. He was held by his neck-ring that he might not attack the people, and he uttered a terrible reiterated cannibal cry. But when he had bitten the corpse, the ecstasy left him, and he was "tamed." . . .

It is obvious that nothing could be more harmless to the community; one useless body per year satisfactorily satisfied the craving for violence which we have clumsily supplied in modern times in the form of oaths, blood-and-thunder, and vows to undertake the death of industrious households. . . .

All these uses of cannibalism are, however, of small moment in comparison [to] . . . its service in the cause of patriotism. Nothing, we are well aware, will so hold in check the hostile elements of a nation as a common purpose of revenge. This may be raised to a high degree of utility by various well-known phrases and figures of oratory which picture our determination to "drink the blood of our enemies." It has however been held essential that we pursue this end by the death, in great numbers and with distressing tortures, of young men in sound health and vigor. Nothing could show more lamentably our ignorance of previous human experiments. It is this aspect of cannibalism that has appealed most widely to the human species; it has enabled them to derive the most intense emotional satisfaction from the death, even the accidental death, of one solitary enemy, allowing them to taste revenge in a thoroughgoing and convincing manner, ministering to their faith in his extirpation, root and branch, body and soul. . . .

The Maoris of New Zealand [for example] before the feast, took from their enemies the exquisitely tattooed heads which were their incomparable pride, and setting them on posts about them, taunted them after this fashion:

"You thought to flee, ha? But my power overtook you.
You were cooked; you were made food for my mouth.
Where is your father? He is cooked.
Where is your brother? He is eaten.
Where is your wife? There she sits, a wife for me!"

No one who is familiar with the breakdown of emotional satisfaction in warfare as it is recorded in postwar literature of our time can fail to see in all this a hopeful device for the re-establishment of an emotional complex which shows every sign of disintegration among us. It is obvious that something must be done, and no suggestion seems more hopeful than this drawn from the Maoris of New Zealand.

The serviceability of cannibalism is therefore well established. In view of the fact that ends now so widely sought in modern war and its aftermaths can thus be attained by the comparatively innocent method of cannibalism, is it not desirable that we consider seriously the possibility of substituting the one for the other before we become involved in another national propaganda? Our well-proved methods of publicity give us a new assurance in the adoption even of unfamiliar programs; where we might at one time well have doubted the possibility of popularizing a practice so unused, we can now venture more boldly. While there is yet time, shall we not choose deliberately between war and cannibalism?[1]

This modest proposal, written about 1925 when Ruth Benedict was, though nearing 40, at the very beginning of her career, and published only out of her *Nachlass* by (who else?) Margaret Mead more than a quarter of a century later, displays the defining characteristics of virtually all her prose: passion, distance, directness, and a relentlessness so complete as to very nearly match that of the giant who is here her model. She did not have Swift's wit, nor the furor of his hatred, and, her cases before her, she did not need his inventiveness. But she had his fixity of purpose and its severity as well.

This vein of iron in Benedict's work, the determined candor of her style, has not, I think, always been sufficiently appreciated. In part, this is perhaps because she was a woman, and women, even professional women, have not been thought inclined to the mordant (though the example

[1]R. Benedict, "The Uses of Cannibalism," in M. Mead, *An Anthropologist at Work: Writings of Ruth Benedict* (Boston, 1959), pp. 44–48. The relevance of this piece and its Swiftian echoes for Benedict's work has been briefly noted before; see J. Boon, *Other Tribes, Other Scribes* (Cambridge, Eng., 1983), p. 110.

of that other Vassarite, Mary McCarthy, might have worked against such an idea). In part it is perhaps a result of the fact that she wrote a fair amount of rather soft-focus lyric poetry and tended to begin and end her works with onward and upward sermons somewhat discontinuous with what the body of the work actually conveyed. And perhaps most of all it has been a result of a conflation of her with the larger-than-life Mead—her student, friend, colleague, and in the end custodian ("proprietor" might be a better term) of her reputation—from whom she could hardly be, on the page, more unlike. But whatever the reason, Benedict's temper, as both her followers and her critics for the most part conceive it—intuitive, gauzy, sanguine, and romantic—is at odds with that displayed in her texts.

The connection with Swift, and beyond him with that highly special mode of social critique of which he is in English the acknowledged master, rests on more than this particular piece of self-conscious impersonation, which may have been written as much to blow off steam as anything else. It rests on Benedict's use, over and over again, from the beginning of her career to its end, and virtually to the exclusion of any other, of the rhetorical strategy upon which that mode of critique centrally depends: the juxtaposition of the all-too-familiar and the wildly exotic in such a way that they change places. In her work as in Swift's (and that of others who have worked in this tradition—Montesquieu, Veblen, Erving Goffman, and a fair number of novelists), the culturally at hand is made odd and arbitrary, the culturally distant, logical and straightforward. Our own forms of life become strange customs of a strange people: those in some far-off land, real or imagined, become expectable behavior given the circumstances. There confounds Here. The Not-us (or Not-U.S.) unnerves the Us.

This strategy of portraying the alien as the familiar with the signs changed is most often referred to as satire. But the term is at once too broad and too narrow. Too broad, because there are other sorts of literary mockery—Martial's, Molière's and James Thurber's. Too narrow, because neither derision nor extravagant humor is necessarily involved. Every so often there is a sardonic remark, very dry and very quiet—"[Zuni] folktales always relate of good men their unwillingness to take office—though they always take it." "Why voluntarily hang yourself from hooks or concentrate on your navel, or never spend your capital?"[2] But the pervading tone in Benedict's works is one of high seriousness and no ridicule at all. Her style is indeed comedic, in the sense that its purpose is the subversion of human pretension, and its attitude is worldly; but it is so in a deadly earnest way. Her ironies are all sincere.

The intrinsically humorous effects that arise from conjoining the beliefs and practices of one's most immediate readers to those of African witches and Indian medicine men (or, as our excerpt shows, of cannibals) are indeed very great; so great that Benedict's success in suppressing them in the works that made her famous, *Patterns of Culture* and *The Chrysanthemum and the Sword*, both of which are organized from beginning to end in a look-unto-ourselves-as-we-would-look-unto-others manner, is the foundation of her achievement as an author-writer "founder of discursivity." "Self-nativising," to invent a general term for this sort of thing, produces cultural horselaughter so naturally and so easily, and has been so consistently thus used, from "Des cannibales," *Lettres persanes*, and *Candide* to *The Mikado*,

[2]R. Benedict, *Patterns of Culture* (New York, 1959), p. 96 (first published, 1932); *The Chrysanthemum and the Sword: Patterns of Japanese Culture* (New York, 1974), p. 228 (first published, 1946).

The Theory of the Leisure Class, and *Henderson the Rain King* (to say nothing of intramural japes like Horace Miner's "Body Ritual Among the Nacirema," or Thomas Gladwin's "Latency and the Equine Subconscious"),[3] that it seems built into the very thing itself. To get it out so as to change parody into portraiture, social sarcasm into moral pleading, as Benedict did, is to work very much against the tropological grain.

It is also to perfect a genre, edificatory ethnography, anthropology designed to improve, that is normally botched either by moral posturing (as in *The Mountain People*), by exaggerated self-consciousness (as in *New Lives for Old*), or by ideological *parti pris* (as in *The Moral Basis of a Backward Society*).[4] The reality of Zuni equanimity or Japanese shamefacedness aside, issues by now pretty well moot, this is a remarkable accomplishment. But what is even more remarkable, it is an accomplishment that arises not out of field work, of which Benedict did little and that indifferent, nor out of systematic theorizing, in which she was scarcely interested. It arises almost entirely out of the development of a powerful expository style at once spare, assured, lapidary, and above all resolute: definite views, definitely expressed. "[A] wood-cut page from an old 15th century Book of Hours," she wrote in her journal, perhaps sometime in the 1920's, "with its honest limitation to the nature of the wood it worked in, can give us a quality of pleasure which the superfluous craftsmanship of [the late nineteenth, early twentieth century white-line wood engraver] Timothy Cole can

[3] H. Miner, "Body Ritual Among the Nacirema," *American Anthropologist,* 58 (1956): 503–13; T. Gladwin, "Latency and the Equine Subconscious," *American Anthropologist,* 64 (1962): 1292–96.
[4] C. Turnbull, *The Mountain People* (New York, 1972); M. Mead, *New Lives for Old: Cultural Transformation of Manus, 1928–53* (New York, 1956); E. Banfield, *The Moral Basis of a Backward Society* (Chicago, 1958).

never touch. And a dozen lines of an etching by Rembrandt, each line bitten visibly into the metal, conjures up a joy and a sense of finality that the whole 19th century does not communicate."[5]

So with words.

《》

So indeed, when words, like wood and metal, are there to begin with. Benedict's style, as she herself as a professional anthropologist, was born adult. It was already in being, more or less in perfected form, in the early specialized studies through which she earned her, once it began, extraordinarily rapid entry to the discipline—and to the institutional center of it, Columbia's commanding heights, at that. The later works, upon which her wider reputation rests, the first published at 47, the second at 59, two years before her death, simply deploy it on a larger scale in a grander manner.

It had, of course, a kind of prehistory in her college writing, in some abortive fragments of feminist biography quickly abandoned when she turned to anthropology, and (though the nature of its relevance is normally misconceived) in her poetry.[6] But as ethnography, her style was invariant from beginning to end: incised lines, bitten with finality.

From 1922:

The Indians of the Plains share with the tribes to the east and west an inordinate pursuit of the vision. Even certain highly formalized conceptions relating to it are found on the Atlantic Coast and on

[5]In Mead, *Anthropologist at Work*, p. 153; the entry is not dated.
[6]For examples of some of these writings, as well as for the misconceptions of them (stemming from an overly autobiographical, the-Real-Ruth reading of them) see J. Modell, *Ruth Benedict: Patterns of a Life* (Philadelphia, 1983); cf. Mead, *Anthropologist at Work*.

the Pacific. Thus, in spite of all diversity of local rulings, the approach to the vision was, or might always be, through isolation and self-mortification. More formally still, the vision, over immense territories, ran by a formula according to which some animal or bird or voice appeared to the suppliant and talked with him, describing the power he bestowed on him, and giving him songs, mementoes, taboos, and perhaps involved ceremonial procedure. Henceforth for this individual this thing that had thus spoken with him at this time became his "guardian spirit."[7]

From 1934:

The Zuni are a ceremonious people, a people who value sobriety and inoffensiveness above all other virtues. Their interest is centered upon the rich and complex ceremonial life. Their cults of the masked gods, of healing, of the sun, of the sacred fetishes, of war, of the dead, are formal and established bodies of ritual with priestly officials and calendric observances. No field of activity competes with ritual for foremost place in their attention.[8]

From 1946:

Any attempt to understand the Japanese must begin with their version of what it means to "take one's proper station." Their reliance upon order and hierarchy and our faith in freedom and equality are poles apart and it is hard for us to give hierarchy its just due as a possible social mechanism. Japan's confidence in hierarchy is basic in her whole notion of man's relation to the State and it is only by describing some of their national institutions like the family, the State, religious and economic life that it is possible for us to understand their view of life.[9]

Whatever this sort of writing is, it is all of a piece: the same thing said and resaid until it seems either as undeniable as the laws of motion or as cooked up as a lawyer's brief; only the examples change. This hedgehog air of hers of being a

[7] R. Benedict, "The Vision in Plains Culture," *American Anthropologist*, 24 (1922): 1–23; quote from p. 1.
[8] *Patterns of Culture*, p. 64.
[9] *The Chrysanthemum and the Sword*, p. 43.

truth-teller with only one truth to tell, but that one fundamental—the Plains Indians are ecstatic, the Zuni are ceremonious, the Japanese are hierarchical (and we are, always,
otherwise)—is what so divides Benedict's professional readers into those who regard her work as magisterial and those
who find it monomaniac. It is also what brought her such an
enormous popular audience. Unlike Mead, who achieved a
somewhat similar result with a loose-limbed, improvisa-
tional style, saying seventeen things at once and marvelously
adaptable to the passing thought, white-line curlicuing if
ever there was such, Benedict found herself a public by sticking determinedly to the point.

The work in which this unlikely meeting of an aesthetic
mind, rather at odds with the world around it, and a prag-
matic mass audience, casting about for useful knowledge,
first occurred is, of course, *Patterns of Culture*. Brief, vivid,
and superbly organized, the book, which has sold nearly two
million copies in more than two dozen languages, clearly
struck a chord, rang a bell, and sent a message. The right text
at the right time.

The literary form of the work is at once so simple, so
compact, and so sharply outlined, that it has proved more or
less impossible even for those most maddened by it ever to
forget it. A conjunction of a triadic descriptive scheme
(three wildly contrasting tribal cultures), a dichotomous
conceptual typology (two drastically opposed sorts of human temperament), and a unitary governing metaphor (alternative life-ways selected from a universal "arc" of available
possibilities), its composition could hardly be more elementary, its structure more overt. Like *Travels into Several Remote Nations of the World* (though that was in four parts, and
had Proportion for a metaphor), it stays in the mind.

III

Benedict's Houyhnhnms, Brobdingnagians, and Ya-
hoos—the Zuni, the Kwakiutl, and the Dobu—provide a
frame for her text that is not so much narrational (plotted
tales imposing an explanatory logic on a train of events) as
presentational (thematic set-pieces imposing a moral color-
ation on a system of practices). *Patterns of Culture* was not
written to be cited. No one goes to it, and I doubt anyone
ever much did, despite the overheated "Is it really so?" de-
bates which arose around it, to settle factual issues about
Pueblo, Northwest Coast, or Melanesian social life. (Two of
her three cases were, of course, unconnected with any field
research of hers. And even in the one with respect to which
she did have some firsthand knowledge, she was not, given
the highly circumscribed nature of her Zuni work, herself
an important source of the material she reviewed.)[10] Benedict trafficked, not only here but just about everywhere in
her work, not in description (there is virtually nothing, folktales aside, of which she is the primary recorder) but in a distinctive sort of redescription: the sort that startles. Her real-
life Luggnaggs and Lilliputs are, like the fictional ones, primarily meant to disconcert.

And so they surely do, either because they reproach us
as the Zuni do (Why can we not be thus cooperative?), car-
icature us as the Kwakiutl do (Is not gaining status by setting
fire to slaves but conspicuous waste writ conspicuously
large?), or accuse us as the Dobu do (Do we not, too, half
believe that "the good man, the successful man, is he who
has cheated another of his place"?).[11] The whole enterprise,
three chapters absolutely crammed with detailed material of
the most curious sort—Zuni passage rites, Kwakiutl chants,

---

[10]See, for the Zuni case, T. N. Pandey, "Anthropologists at Zuni," *Proceedings of the American Philosophical Society*, 116 (Aug. 1972): 321–37.
[11]*Patterns of Culture*, p. 130.

Dobu residence arrangements—has the air, the same one that remorseless descriptions of Blefuscu judicial procedures or Laputian linguistics have, of being concerned with something else, and somewhere else, rather closer to home. The whole thing is done with a progression of pointed contrasts in which the constant opposing term, the one that is pointed at, is—a reminding allusion now and then aside—eloquently absent. Not mere allegory, deep meanings secreted within Aesopean fables, but negative-space writing. What is there, bold and definite, constructs what isn't: our cannibal face.

Around this dominant trope—extravagant otherness as self-critique, we have met the Not-us and they are not-Us—are gathered, in the five short thesis-driving chapters that bracket the three long ethnographic ones, the more obvious and more mechanical Apollonian/Dionysian and arc-of-selection images. They are supposed, these clanking metaphors, to make the point fully explicit. But it is one of the ironies that haunt Benedict's work, along with the misassimilation of it to that of Mead and the misconception of it as documentational, that they have served in the event mainly to obscure it. Sometimes, less *is* more. Trying too hard to be clear, as someone who had been a poet ought to have known, can dim an argument best left oblique.

Benedict's Apollonian/Dionysian contrast—"[He who] keeps the middle of the road, stays within the known map" vs. "[He who] seeks to . . . escape from the bounds imposed on him by his five senses, to break through into another order of experience" (p. 79)—is taken, of course, though not with much else, from Nietzsche's *The Birth of Tragedy*. The arc-of-selection metaphor is taken, also with not much else, from phonology—"In cultural life as it is in speech, selection [from the inventory of physically available possibilities] is the prime necessity" (p. 34)—and capsulated in the famous Digger Indian proverb that serves as epigraph to the book: "In the beginning God gave to every people a cup of clay and from this cup they drank their life" (pp. xvi, 33). Between them, these two figures, the one of temperamental extremes, radically incommensurable, the other of a range of choices, mutually exclusive, are designed to rescue the ethnographic material from its radical particularity; to make what is singular in its description general in its implications. Science through poetry—the study of "primitive civilizations" is to be the foundation for an analysis of culture as exact as biology:

The understanding we need of our own cultural processes can most economically be arrived at by a détour. When the historical relations of human beings and their immediate forbears in the animal kingdom were too involved to use in establishing the fact of biological evolution, Darwin made use instead of the structure of beetles, and the process, which in the complex physical organization of the human is confused, in the simpler material was transparent in its cogency. It is the same in the study of cultural mechanisms. We need all the enlightenment we can obtain from the study of thought and behavior as it is organized in the less complicated groups. (pp. 60–61)

This sorting out of beetles (a surprising image for a scholar so humanistically oriented to choose) leads however not to a narrativist representation of cultural variation of the sort one would expect from an anthropological Darwin, a historical story with a scientific plot, but to an attempt to construct a catalog of genres, cultural kinds appropriately named. Benedict is not really after "processes" or "mechanisms" (nor—some generalized remarks, more hortatory than analytical, about "integration" and "abnormality" aside—does she offer any); rather she seeks, once again, ways of making difference tell. The problem is that, in promising otherwise, she seems to have insured herself of being understood as testing out a theory when what she really was doing (and knew that she was doing) was pressing home a critique: "The recognition of cultural relativity," the famous—or infamous—last paragraph of the book runs,

carries with it its own values. . . . It challenges customary opinions and causes those who have been bred to them acute discomfort. It rouses pessimism because it throws old formulae into confusion. . . . [But as] soon as the new opinion is embraced as customary belief, it will be another trusted bulwark of the good life. We shall arrive then at a more realistic social faith, accepting as grounds of hope and as new bases for tolerance the coexisting and equally valid patterns of life which mankind has created for itself from the raw materials of existence. (pp. 239–40)

That someone so intent to disturb should so represent herself as engaged in constructing a *table raisonnée* of human possibilities is mainly to be accounted for by the intellectual environment in which she worked, but to which, coming late and with a metaphorical turn of mind, she never quite properly belonged. Between the wars, the conception of anthropology as uniquely positioned to find out the essentials of social life that are disguised or covered over in complex, modern societies reached perhaps its greatest peak, though it of course existed before in Durkheim (*"les formes élémentaires"*) and has hung on after in Lévi-Strauss (*"les structures élémentaires"*). Franz Boas, Paul Radin, Robert Lowie, Margaret Mead, and Edward Sapir in the United States, Bronislaw Malinowski, A. R. Radcliffe-Brown, A. C. Haddon, and C. C. Seligman in Britain all shared it and the image of primitive societies as "natural laboratories," anthropology's Galapagos, that went with it. But it fits ill with the view of such societies as fun-house mirrorings—this one elongated, that one squashed, the other twisted—of our own that was at the imaginative center of Benedict's sensibility.

The attempt to be (or anyway to look like) a "real scientist," as that beatific state was then conceived, is what led to the two-bucket typology, the curveless arc, and to that disastrous final sentence about "equally valid patterns of life," which, as Elgin Williams pointed out years ago, contradicts everything that is conveyed by the substance of the book.[12] In time, she at least half realized this and pulled herself free of methodological conceits she did not believe to produce (one unfortunate—and again, unfortunately memorable—chapter aside) the book most surely her own, and, though it has sold "only" 350,000 copies, the most certainly lasting: *The Chrysanthemum and the Sword*.

《》

The Western Imagination, to the degree one can talk intelligibly about such a vast and elusive entity at all, has tended to construct rather different representations for itself of the otherness of others as it has come into practical contact with one or another sort of them. Africa, the Heart of Darkness: tom-toms, witchcraft, unspeakable rites. Asia, the Decaying Mansion: effete brahmins, corrupt mandarins, dissolute emirs. Aboriginal Australia, Oceania, and in part the Americas, Humanity *degré zéro*: ur-kinship, ur-religion, ur-science, and the origins of incest. But Japan, about the last such elsewhere located, or anyway penetrated, has been for us more absolutely otherwise. It has been the Impossible Object. An enormous something, trim, intricate, and madly

[12]E. Williams, "Anthropology for the Common Man," *American Anthropologist*, 49 (1947): 84–90. For some general discussions of "the problem of relativism" (which I think a pseudo-problem), see C. Geertz, "Anti Anti-Relativism," *American Anthropologist*, 86 (1984): 263–78, and "The Uses of Diversity," in S. McMurrin, ed., *The Tanner Lectures on Human Values*, vol. 7 (Cambridge, Eng., 1986), pp. 253–75.

busy, that, like an Escher drawing, fails to compute. From *Madama Butterfly* and *Kokoro* to *Pacific Overtures* and *L'Empire des signes*, the country (the only real place, save of course for England, that appears as more than a reference point in *Gulliver's Travels*) has looked not just distant but off the map: "a funny place." "The Japanese," Benedict's book opens, "[are] the most alien enemy the United States [has] ever fought"—a challenge not just to our power, but to our powers of comprehension. "Conventions of war which Western nations had come to accept as a fact of human nature obviously did not exist for the Japanese. [This] made the war in the Pacific more than a series of landings on island beaches, more than an unsurpassed problem of logistics. It made it a major problem in the nature of the enemy. We had to understand their behavior in order to cope with it" (p. 1).

The great originality of Benedict's book (which had its genesis, of course, in her intelligence and propaganda work during the war) and the basis of its force, a force even its severest critics have felt, lies in the fact that she does not seek to unriddle Japan and the Japanese by moderating this sense of an oddly made world populated by oddly wired people, but by accentuating it. The habit of contrasting an "as-we-know" us with an "imagine-that" them is here carried to climax; as though American Indians and Melanesians had been but warm-ups for the *really* different. And what is more, the contrasting is now explicit and particular, not, as in *Patterns of Culture*, implied and general—specific this-es set against specific thats. I had thought to count the number of such "in America" / "in Japan" tropes in *The Chrysanthemum and the Sword*, but soon gave it up as a tiresome task leading to an unscalable number. But the drumbeat of them resounds, instance upon instance, through the whole of the book.

On sleeping:

Sleeping is . . . one of the most accomplished arts of the Japanese. They sleep with complete relaxation . . . under circumstances we regard as sheer impossibilities. This has surprised many Western students of the Japanese. Americans make insomnia almost a synonym for psychic tenseness, and according to our standards there are high tensions in the Japanese character. . . . Americans are used to rating sleeping as something one does to keep up one's strength and the first thought of most of us when we wake up in the morning is to calculate how many hours we slept that night. The length of our slumbers tells us how much energy and efficiency we will have that day. The Japanese sleep for other reasons. (pp. 181–82)

On eating:

According to Japanese ideas, involuntary deprivation of food is an especially good test of how 'hardened' one is. . . . [Being] without food is a chance to demonstrate that one can 'take it.' . . . [One's] strength is raised by one's victory of the spirit, not lowered by the lack of calories and vitamins. The Japanese do not recognize the one-to-one correspondence which Americans postulate between body nourishment and body strength. (p. 182)

On sex and marriage:

They fence off one province which belongs to the wife from another which belongs to erotic pleasure. Both provinces are equally open and above board. The two are not divided from each other as in American life by the fact that one is what a man admits to the public and the other is surreptitious. . . . The Japanese set up no ideal, as we do in the United States, which pictures love and marriage as one and the same thing. (p. 184)

On masculinity:

[Homosexuality falls] among those 'human feelings' about which moralistic attitudes are inappropriate. It must be kept in its proper place and not interfere with carrying on the family. Therefore the danger of a man . . . 'becoming' a homosexual, as the Western phrase has it, is hardly conceived. . . . The Japanese are especially shocked at adult passive homosexuals in the United States. Adult men in Japan would seek out boy partners, for adults consider the passive rôle to be beneath their dignity. The Japanese draw their own lines as to what a man can do and retain his self-respect, but they are not the ones we draw. (p. 188)

On drinking:

The Japanese consider our American total abstinence pledges as one of the strange vagaries of the Occident. . . . Drinking *sake* is a pleasure no man in his right mind would deny himself. But alcohol belongs among the minor relaxations and no man in his right mind, either, would become obsessed by it. According to their way of thinking one does not fear to 'become' a drunkard any more than one fears to 'become' a homosexual, and it is true that the compulsive drunkard is not a social problem in Japan. (p. 189)

On Good and Evil:

To American ears such doctrines [that no evil is inherent in man's soul; that virtue does not consist in fighting evil] seem to lead to a philosophy of self-indulgence and licence. The Japanese, however . . . define the task of life as fulfilling one's obligations. They fully accept the fact that repaying [moral debts] means sacrificing one's personal desires and pleasures. The idea that the pursuit of happiness is a serious goal of life is to them an amazing and immoral doctrine. (p. 192)

And on happy endings:

[The] 'happy ending' is . . . rare in their novels and plays. American popular audiences crave solutions. They want to believe that people live happily ever after. They want to know that people are rewarded for their virtue. . . . Japanese popular audiences sit dissolved in tears watching the hero come to his tragic end and the lovely heroine slain because of a turn of the wheel of fortune. Such plots are the high points of an evening's entertainment. They are what people go to see. . . . Their modern war films are in the same tradition. Americans who see these movies often say that they are the best pacifist propaganda they ever saw. This is a characteristic American reaction because the movies are wholly concerned with the sacrifice and suffering of war. . . . Their curtain scenes are not victory or even banzai charges. They are overnight halts in some featureless Chinese town deep in the mud. Or they show maimed, halt and blind representatives of three generations of a Japanese family, survivors of three wars. . . . The stirring background of Anglo-American 'Cavalcade' movies is all absent. . . . Not even the purposes for which the war was fought are mentioned. It is enough for the Japanese audience that all the people on the screen have repaid [their moral debt to the Emperor] with everything that was in them, and these movies therefore in Japan were propaganda of the militarists. Their sponsors knew that Japanese audiences were not stirred by them to pacifism. (pp. 192–94)

The empirical validity of these various assertions, taken from a mere ten pages, not unrepresentative, in the middle of the book, aside (and some of them do sound more like reports from a society supposed than from one surveyed), the unrelenting piling up of them, the one hardly dispatched before the next appears, is what gives Benedict's argument its extraordinary energy. She persuades, to the degree she does persuade—significantly so, in fact, even among the Japanese, who seem to find themselves as puzzling as does everyone else—by the sheer force of iteration. The Us/Not-us motif is pursued through an enormous range of wildly assorted materials derived from wildly assorted sources (legends, movies, interviews with Japanese expatriates and prisoners of war, scholarly works, newspaper accounts, radio broadcasts, "antiquarian papers," novels, speeches in the Diet, military intelligence reports) with the sort of single-mindedness that compels either general belief or an equally general skepticism. Prevented, and not only by the war, but by deafness and disinclination, from "being there" literally, Benedict rests her authority on being there imaginatively— moving locus to locus across the Impossible Object, and confronting on every page what she herself calls "the ever-present question: What is 'wrong with this picture?'" (p. 7).

But, as one can see even from this short sequence of quotations, moving from examples in which "they" sound the odd case to ones in which "we" do, a disconcerting twist appears in the course of this forced march through cultural difference; an unexpected swerve that sets the campaign a bit off course. It comes in the fact that, as she proceeds through everything from Japanese incredulity that an American admiral should be awarded a medal for rescuing crippled warships to American incredulity that the Japanese can see fulfillment in suicide, Japan comes to look, somehow, less and less erratic and arbitrary while the United States comes to look, somehow, more and more so. There is, in fact, nothing "wrong with the picture," just with those who look at it upside down; and the enemy who at the beginning of the book is the most alien we have ever fought is, by the end of it, the most reasonable we have ever conquered. Japanese newspapers pronounce defeat as "all to the good for the ultimate salvation of Japan." Japanese politicians happily govern the country under MacArthur's umbrella-parasol. And the Emperor, urged by the General's advisors to disavow divinity, complains he is not really regarded as a god but does so anyway because foreigners seem to think that he is and it should be good for the country's image.

This peculiar passage from perversity to pragmatism on the Asian hand and from levelheadedness to provinciality on the American, rigidity and flexibility passing one another somewhere in mid-Pacific, is the real story *The Chrysanthemum and the Sword* has to tell, though again it tells it more in the form of an examples-and-morals homily than in that of a directionally plotted tale. What started out as a familiar sort of attempt to unriddle oriental mysteries ends up, only too successfully, as a deconstruction, *avant la lettre*, of occidental clarities. At the close, it is, as it was in *Patterns of*

Culture, us that we wonder about. On what, pray tell, do our certainties rest? Not much, apparently, save that they're ours.

《》

So, again, and here more powerfully because more confidently (if, in *Patterns of Culture* she writes like a lawyer pleading a case, in *The Chrysanthemum and the Sword* she writes like a judge deciding one), Benedict dismantles American exceptionalism by confronting it with that—even more exceptional—of a spectacularized other. But again, too, the fact that that is what she in fact is doing, intends to be doing, and in the event gets pretty well done, is somewhat obscured, to the point that it is frequently not seen at all. And it is the same interpretive misstep, similarly encouraged by Benedict herself, her own best misreader, that causes all the trouble: the misassimilation of her work to the intellectual environment immediately surrounding it.

Benedict's courage, extraordinary when you think about it, in writing about the Japanese as she did, a few years after Pearl Harbor, the Bataan Death March, Guadalcanal, and a thousand Hollywood movies populated with myopic sadists lisping hatred, has been at least occasionally remarked; but the subversive effect of her doing so on her American readers' received views about which way is forward and which direction is up (something even riskier) has not. Although undergraduates, not yet appropriately instructed as to what one is not allowed to look for in an anthropological monograph, sometimes sense the book's satirical edge, and are disturbed by it, the common conception of the work has been that it amounts to a psycho-political how-to-handle-the-Japanese training manual, conceptually a bit flighty, empirically a bit weak, morally a bit dubious. What is surely one of the most acid ethnographies ever written—"[The Japanese] play up suicide as the Americans play up crime, and they have the same vicarious enjoyment of it" (p. 167)—and the most bleakly mocking—"[A Japanese's moral debts] are [his] constant shadow, like a New York farmer's worry about his mortgage or a Wall Street financier's as he watches the market climb when he has sold short" (p. 115)—is seen as a brief for a science and sensibility, can-do optimism.

That was certainly the context, intellectual and political (or, as this was wartime and just after, intellectual-political), within which the book was written. Now it was not the natural laboratory, *"formes élémentaires,"* behold-the-beetle image of what anthropology had "to contribute" that Benedict felt was necessary in order to raise her work above the level of mere *belles lettres* into something more scientifically respectable. Rather, now it was "national character," "policy science," and "culture at a distance." And the people around her now were not just the inevitable Margaret Mead, herself turned toward larger canvases and more strategic goals, but a whole phalanx of psychological warriors, propaganda analysts, intelligence experts, and program planners. Scholars in uniform.

The story of this particular phase in American social science (and it was a phase; by the late 1950's it was over, anyway in anthropology, killed by too much promising of elephants and bringing forth of mice) has yet to be written in a detached and analytical way. There are only anecdotes, puffs, and war-horse reminiscences. But the fact that Benedict was not altogether at home with its style, its purposes, and its cast of mind, what she herself might have called its temper, is clear. Here, too, what she says when she is talking about her subject and what she says when she is talking about why she is talking about her subject don't quite comport.

Because *The Chrysanthemum and the Sword*, like *Patterns of Culture*, only really gets started about fifty pages in and is essentially over about fifty from its close (Benedict's works, like most Moralities, seem naturally to climax at their center) this two-mindedness appears most obviously again in the opening and closing sections of the book. The first chapter, "Assignment: Japan," a drum roll, and the last, "The Japanese Since VJ-Day," a briefing paper, place the work with the appropriate breathlessness in the Science-in-the-Nation's-Service frame that the times seemed to call for: "Whether the issue [facing the U.S. Government] was military or diplomatic, whether it was raised by questions of high policy or of leaflets to be dropped behind the Japanese front lines, every insight was important" (p. 4). But it is in the penultimate chapter, "The Child Learns," that the intellectual style of the Foreign Morale Analysis Division of the Office of War Information and its Navy-sponsored civilian successor, Columbia University Research in Contemporary Cultures, most fatally invades Benedict's crisscross world. The apostrophes to the anthropology of leaflets and high policy have faded with the excitements that gave rise to them; but, like the pages on relativism in *Patterns of Culture*, those on shame, guilt, swaddling, and teasing in *The Chrysanthemum and the Sword* have had only too much staying power.

Whatever the reasons this shy, courtly, rather depressive, rather disdainful, and anything but right-minded woman may have had for wanting to surround an aesthetic view of human behavior with the trappings of an activist social science (a sense of being out of step, a desire to connect, a will to believe, a Christian idealism even anthropology couldn't cure), they are lost in the mists of her personal life.

That she was not altogether comfortable in doing so can be seen, however, in the sudden shift in the child-raising chapter from a confident descriptive idiom to a much less confident causal one. In the compact, close-focus middle chapters on Japanese conceptions of hierarchy, moral indebtedness, "the circle of feelings," and self-discipline, everything is a matter of a point in a pattern, the placing of some practice or perception or belief or value in a context such that it makes sense; or anyway, Japanese sense. In "The Child Learns," the longest and most rambling chapter in the book, the project turns to a search for *mechanisms*, for specific socialization practices that will induce, as heat induces boiling or infection scarring, psychological dispositions that can account for why it is that the Japanese "cannot stand ridicule," dislike unpruned gardens, put mirrors in their shrines, and regard their gods as benevolent. A discourse on forms becomes, confusedly, one on levers.

The levers involved are, of course, familiar, not to say notorious—heavy diapers, taunting mothers, peer group tyranny. But what is interesting is that they are, in a book otherwise so intellectually self-reliant as to seem hermetic, for the most part not hers. The swaddling business, which is passed over rather hurriedly as a matter of fact, comes of course from Geoffrey Gorer, the English enthusiast Mead brought into the Columbia and Washington circle after Bateson's withdrawal from it, and whom Benedict almost eloquently omits from her generous "Acknowledgements," though she does, rather coolly, cite him as having "also emphasized the role of Japanese toilet training." The teasing business (the child alternately abandoned and embraced), of which much more is made, comes from Bateson and Mead's 1942 monograph on Bali, where it is the pervading theme.

And the peer group business comes again from a wartime report of Gorer's, this time at least briefly quoted.[13]

The externality to Benedict's book of these borrowed devices, awkwardly introduced and clumsily applied, can be seen in the progression of the chapter itself, as it moves uneasily past them to return, almost with a sigh of relief, to portraiture—cherry blossoms, tea ceremonies, the lacquered lives of Japanese men—toward its conclusion. But perhaps the most telling picture of the tension comes again from Margaret Mead. In her book on Benedict and her writings, which is mainly an attempt, a decade after Benedict's death, to incorporate the older woman's persona into her own—making a predecessor look like a successor with a vengeance—Mead describes, in an exasperated and even resentful tone, unique in a book otherwise hagiographic, why it was *The Chrysanthemum and the Sword* achieved the acceptance it did:

Ruth Benedict herself was completely converted to the usefulness for the safety of the world, of the methods she had used. Certain other expositions of these same methods had antagonized readers because they had so bared their methods of deriving the insights that they reverberated uncomfortably in the minds of the readers. Her own lack of dependence upon psychoanalytic methods—which, in this case, meant a lack of dependence upon the zones of the body, which never made any sense to her—made the book palatable to readers who had resisted, as they now praised, the insights about the Japanese emperor originally developed by Geoffrey Gorer in 1942. Furthermore, her basic skepticism about American culture, which she shared with most liberals of her generation, made it possible for liberals to accept her sympathetic un-

[13]G. Gorer, *Themes in Japanese Culture*, Transactions of the New York Academy of Science, 5 (1943): 106–24; *The Chrysanthemum and the Sword*, p. 259. G. Bateson and M. Mead, *Balinese Character* (New York, 1942). G. Gorer, *Japanese Character Structure* (New York, 1943); *The Chrysanthemum and the Sword*, p. 274.

derstanding of the virtues of Japanese culture without feeling forced to take a similarly sympathetic attitude toward their own culture, and this removed a stumbling block which stood in the way of anthropologists who did not feel this skepticism so strongly. It was the kind of book that colonels could mention to generals and captains to admirals without fear of producing an explosion against "jargon," the kind of book it would be safe to put in the hands of congressmen alert to resist the "schemes of long-haired intellectuals." The points were made so gracefully, so cogently, that the book disarmed almost all possible enemies except for those who leaned heavily to the Left and those who, through many years, had formed very clear and usually imperfect notions of their own Japanese experiences—the sort of people we used, in another context, to call "old China hands."[14]

With anthropological authoring, as with other things, then, it all depends on the company you keep. Having decided what sort of discourse community she and thus Benedict, her John-the-Baptist, should belong to, Mead labors so desperately to keep her from escaping it because she seems to sense, and to sense that others sense, how insecurely Benedict rests there, how very less than complete that "conversion" to save-the-world anthropology in fact was, and how easily the image of ethnography for admirals slips away when one looks at what is there upon the page. Taking Benedict out of that community is, like putting her in, thus an interpretive act, and, if I may say so before someone else does, a contentious one with ambitions of its own.

To say one should read Benedict not with the likes of Gorer, Mead, Alexander Leighton, or Lawrence Frank at the back of one's mind, but with Swift, Montesquieu, Veblen, and W. S. Gilbert, is to urge a particular understanding of what it is she is saying. *The Chrysanthemum and the Sword* is no more a prettied up science-without-tears policy tract than

[14]Mead, *Anthropologist at Work*, p. 428.

Travels Into Several Remote Nations of the World, In Four Parts, By Lemuel Gulliver, First a Surgeon and Then a Captain of Several Ships is a children's book. Benedict, who actually hardly went anywhere either, also wrote, as Swift said that he did, "to vex the world rather than divert it." It would be rather a pity were the world not to notice it.

6.

BEING HERE

Whose Life Is It Anyway?

Right away this afternoon I go with Abba Jérome to see [the Ethiopian woman] Emawayish and give her pens, ink, and a notebook so she can record for herself—or dictate to her son—the manuscript [of her songs], letting it be understood that the head of the expedition, if he is pleased, will present her with the desired gift.

Emawayish's words this afternoon when I told her, speaking of her manuscript, that it would be especially good for her to write down some love songs like those of the other night: *Does poetry exist in France?* And then: *Does love exist in France?*[1]

However far from the groves of academe anthropologists seek out their subjects—a shelved beach in Polynesia, a charred plateau in Amazonia; Akobo, Meknes, Panther Burn—they write their accounts with the world of lecterns, libraries, blackboards, and seminars all about them. This is the world that produces anthropologists, that licenses them to do the kind of work they do, and within which the kind

[1]M. Leiris, "Phantom Africa," J. Clifford, trans., *Sulfur 15* (1986): 43. The first bracket is my own, the second is the translator's, and the italics are in the original. Clifford translated only a part of Leiris, *L'Afrique fantôme* (Paris, 1934).

129

of work they do must find a place if it is to count as worth attention. In itself, Being There is a postcard experience ("I've been to Katmandu—have you?"). It is Being Here, a scholar among scholars, that gets your anthropology read . . . published, reviewed, cited, taught.

There is nothing particularly new in this; the wealthy eccentrics have been pretty well gone from ethnography since the 1920's, and the connoisseurs, the consultants, and the travel writers have never quite made it in (a few missionaries have, but dressed as professors, usually German). That there is some sort of chair or other under every anthropologist, Collège de France to All Souls, University College to Morningside Heights, seems by now part of the natural order of things. There are a few more completely academicized professions, perhaps—paleography and the study of lichens—but not many.

However, though the fact that almost all ethnographers are university types of one sort or another is so familiar as to confound the thought that matters might be otherwise, the incongruities implicit in such a divided existence—a few years, now and again, scuffling about with cattle herders or yam gardeners, a lifetime lecturing to classes and arguing with colleagues—have recently begun to be more sharply felt. The gap between engaging others where they are and representing them where they aren't, always immense but not much noticed, has suddenly become extremely visible. What once seemed only technically difficult, getting "their" lives into "our" works, has turned morally, politically, even epistemologically, delicate. The *suffisance* of Lévi-Strauss, the assuredness of Evans-Pritchard, the brashness of Malinowski, and the imperturbability of Benedict now seem very far away.

What is at hand is a pervasive nervousness about the

whole business of claiming to explain enigmatical others on the grounds that you have gone about with them in their native habitat or combed the writings of those who have. This nervousness brings on, in turn, various responses, variously excited: deconstructive attacks on canonical works, and on the very idea of canonicity as such; *Ideologiekritik* unmaskings of anthropological writings as the continuation of imperialism by other means; clarion calls to reflexivity, dialogue, heteroglossia, linguistic play, rhetorical self-consciousness, performative translation, verbatim recording, and first-person narrative as forms of cure.[2] The Emawayish question now is everywhere: What happens to reality when it is shipped abroad?

Both the world that anthropologists for the most part study, which once was called primitive, tribal, traditional, or folk and now is called emergent, modernizing, peripheral, or submerged, and the one that they for the most part study it from, academia, have vastly changed from what they were in the days of Dimdim and Dirty Dick on the one hand and Columbia Research in Contemporary Cultures on the other. The end of colonialism altered radically the nature of the social relationship between those who ask and look and those who are asked and looked at. The decline of faith in brute fact, set procedures, and unsituated knowledge in the hu-

[2]For an interesting collection of the very good and the very bad, the knowledgeable and the pretentious, the truly original and the merely dazed, see now J. Clifford and G. Marcus, eds., *Writing Culture: The Poetics and Politics of Ethnography* (Berkeley, Calif., 1986). For a somewhat breathless review, see G. Marcus and M. Fischer, *Anthropology as Cultural Critique: An Experimental Moment in the Human Sciences* (Chicago, 1986). Other recent straws in the same wind include: J. Fabian, *Time and the Other: How Anthropology Makes Its Object* (New York, 1983); J. Clifford, "On Ethnographic Authority," *Representations*, 2 (1983): 118–46; J. Ruby, ed., *A Crack in the Mirror: Reflexive Perspectives in Anthropology* (Philadelphia, 1982); T. Asad, ed., *Anthropology and the Colonial Encounter* (New York, 1973); and D. Hymes, ed., *Reinventing Anthropology* (New York, 1974; first published, 1969).

man sciences, and indeed in scholarship generally, altered no less radically the askers' and lookers' conception of what it was they were trying to do. Imperialism in its classical form, metropoles and possessions, and Scientism in its, impulsions and billiard balls, fell at more or less the same time. Things have been less simple since, on both the Being There and the Being Here sides of the anthropological equation, an equation First World trinkets and Third World songs now more mock than balance.

《》

The transformation, partly juridical, partly ideological, partly real, of the people anthropologists mostly write about, from colonial subject to sovereign citizens, has (whatever the ironies involved in Uganda, Libya, or Kampuchea) altered entirely the moral context within which the ethnographical act takes place. Even those exemplary elsewheres—Lévi-Strauss's Amazon or Benedict's Japan—that were not colonies, but stranded hinterlands or closed-off emperies "in the middle of the sea," stand in a quite different light since Partition, Lumumba, Suez, and Vietnam changed the political grammar of the world. The more recent scattering of encapsulated peoples across the globe— Algerians in France, Koreans in Kuwait, Pakistanis in London, Cubans in Miami—has only extended the process by reducing the spacing of variant turns of mind, as has, of course, jet-plane tourism as well. One of the major assumptions upon which anthropological writing rested until only yesterday, that its subjects and its audience were not only separable but morally disconnected, that the first were to be described but not addressed, the second informed but not implicated, has fairly well dissolved. The world has its compartments still, but the passages between them are much more numerous and much less well secured.

This inter-confusion of object and audience, as though Gibbon were to find himself suddenly with a Roman readership, or M. Homais were to publish essays on "The Depiction of Provincial Life in *Madame Bovary*" in *La Revue des Deux Mondes*, leaves contemporary anthropologists in some uncertainty as to rhetorical aim. Who is now to be persuaded? Africanists or Africans? Americanists or American Indians? Japanologists or Japanese? And of what: Factual accuracy? Theoretical sweep? Imaginative grasp? Moral depth? It is easy enough to answer, "All of the above." It is not quite so easy to produce a text that thus responds.

Indeed, the very right to write—to write ethnography—seems at risk. The entrance of once colonialized or castaway peoples (wearing their own masks, speaking their own lines) onto the stage of global economy, international high politics, and world culture has made the claim of the anthropologist to be a tribune for the unheard, a representer of the unseen, a kenner of the misconstrued, increasingly difficult to sustain. Malinowski's happy "Eureka!" when first coming upon the Trobrianders—"Feeling of ownership: It is I who will describe them . . . [I who will] create them"—sounds in a world of OPEC, ASEAN, *Things Fall Apart*, and Tongan running backs with the Washington Redskins (as well as one of Yoruban, Sinhalese, and Tewa anthropologists) not merely presumptuous, but outright comic. "[What] has become irreducibly curious," the meta-ethnographer James Clifford has written (though perhaps what he meant to say was "dubious"), "is no longer the other, but cultural description itself."[3]

It has become curious (or dubious, or exploitative, or oppressive, or brutal—the adjectives escalate) because most

[3]B. Malinowski, *A Diary in the Strict Sense of the Term* (New York, 1967), p. 150. J. Clifford, "DADA DATA," *Sulfur 16* (1987): 162–64.

anthropologists now writing find themselves in a profession that was largely formed in an historical context—the Colonial Encounter—of which they have no experience and want none. The desire to distance themselves from the power asymmetries upon which that encounter rested, in anthropology as in everything else (and which, however changed in form, have hardly disappeared), is generally quite strong, sometimes overmastering, and produces an attitude toward the very idea of ethnography at least ambivalent:

[Those] ritually repetitive confrontations with the Other which we call fieldwork may be but special instances of the general struggle between the West and its Other. A persistent myth shared by imperialists and many (Western) critics of imperialism alike has been that of a single decisive conquista, occupation, or establishment of colonial power, a myth which has its complement in similar notions of sudden decolonization and accession to independence. Both have worked against giving proper theoretical importance to overwhelming evidence for *repeated* acts of oppression, campaigns of pacification and suppression of rebellions, no matter whether these were carried out by military means, by religious and educational indoctrination, by administrative measures, or, as is more common now, by intricate monetary and economic manipulations under the cover of foreign aid. . . . We cannot exclude the possibility, to say the very least, that repetitive enactment of field research by thousands of aspiring and established practitioners of anthropology has been part of a sustained effort to maintain a certain type of relation between the West and its Other.[4]

Not all the statements are so crude as this, nor so peremptory. But the mood projected ("[There] is now real reason to fear for the future of anthropology. The end of imperialism . . . will mean the end of what has been anthropology," as another viewer with alarm and a program has put

[4]Fabian, *Time and the Other*, p. 149; parenthesis and italics in original.

it)[5] is familiar to the point of leitmotif. In anthropology, as in Faulkner's South, the past is not only not dead, it is not even past; returned field workers trying to write their way out of the job of ordering the "relation between the West and its Other" are as common as ones trying to write their way into it used to be. What job they are to have instead, though there are suggestions ranging from turning anthropology inward upon the mystifications of Western society to scattering it outward across the international hodgepodge of postmodern culture, is less clear.

All of this is made the more dire, leading to distracted cries of plight and crisis, by the fact that at the same time as the moral foundations of ethnography have been shaken by decolonization on the Being There side, its epistemological foundations have been shaken by a general loss of faith in received stories about the nature of representation, ethnographic or any other, on the Being Here side. Confronted, in the academy, by a sudden explosion of polemical prefixes (neo-, post-, meta-, anti-) and subversive title forms (*After Virtue*, *Against Method*, *Beyond Belief*), anthropologists have had added to their "Is it decent?" worry (Who are *we* to describe *them?*) an "Is it possible?" one (Can Ethiopian love be sung in France?), with which they are even less well prepared to deal. How you know you know is not a question they have been used to asking in other than practical, empiricist terms: What is the evidence? How was it collected? What does it show? How words attach to the world, texts to experience, works to lives, is not one they have been used to asking at all.

They are, at least those among them not content to re-

[5] W. S. Willis, Jr., "Skeletons in the Anthropological Closet," in Hymes, *Reinventing Anthropology*, p. 146; I have suppressed a paragraph break.

hearse habitual skills, beginning to get used to asking this question now; and some, a bit unsteadily, are even trying to answer it, if only because if they don't, others—linguists, semioticists, philosophers, and worst of all literary critics—will do it for them:

The whole point of "evoking" rather than "representing" [as an ideal for ethnographic discourse] is that it frees ethnography from *mimesis* and the inappropriate mode of scientific rhetoric that entails "objects," "facts," "descriptions," "inductions," "generalizations," "verification," "experiment," "truth," and like concepts that, except as empty invocations, have no parallels either in the experience of ethnographic fieldwork or in the writing of ethnographies. The urge to conform to the canons of scientific rhetoric has made the easy realism of natural history the dominant mode of ethnographic prose, but it has been an illusory realism, promoting, on the one hand, the absurdity of "describing" nonentities such as "culture" or "society" as if they were fully observable, though somewhat ungainly, bugs, and, on the other, the equally ridiculous behaviorist pretense of "describing" repetitive patterns of action in isolation from the discourse that actors use in constituting and situating their action, and all in simpleminded surety that the observers' grounding discourse is itself an objective form sufficient to the task of describing acts. The problem with the realism of natural history is not, as is often claimed, the complexity of the so-called object of observation, nor failure to apply sufficiently rigorous and replicable methods, nor even less the seeming intractability of the language of description. It is instead a failure of the whole visualist ideology of referential discourse, with its rhetoric of "describing," "comparing," "classifying," and "generalizing," and its presumption of representational signification. In ethnography there are no "things" there to be the objects of a description, the original appearance that the language of description "represents" as indexical objects for comparison, classification, and generalization; there is rather a discourse, and that too, no thing, despite the misguided claims of such translational methods of ethnography as structuralism, ethno-science, and dialogue, which attempt to represent either native discourse or its unconscious patterns, and thus commit the crime of natural history in the mind.[6]

This is rather grand for such a rough and ready discipline as anthropology, and not altogether coherent. But however pumped up and however febrile (Tyler goes on to pronounce ethnography "an occult document . . . an enigmatic, paradoxical, and esoteric conjunction of reality and fantasy . . . a fantasy reality of a reality fantasy"), his argument reflects a recognition, increasingly widespread, that "telling it like it is" is hardly more adequate a slogan for ethnography than for philosophy since Wittgenstein (or Gadamer), history since Collingwood (or Ricoeur), literature since Auerbach (or Barthes), painting since Gombrich (or Goodman), politics since Foucault (or Skinner), or physics since Kuhn (or Hesse). Whether or not "evoking" will solve the problem, whether or not paradox will locate it, there fairly clearly *is* a problem.

This small shower of dropping names, which could easily be whipped into a tropical downpour if one looked across the whole scene of methodological soul-searching in the arts and sciences, suggests ("evokes," perhaps) the dimensions of the problem that ethnographers, virtually all of whom have at least a lingering affection for "facts, descriptions, inductions, and truth," now confront. The pervasive questioning of standard modes of text construction—and standard modes of reading—not only leaves easy realism less easy; it leaves it less persuasive. Whether or not "natural history" is a crime in the mind, it no longer seems quite so natural, either to those who read it or to those who write it. Besides the moral hypochondria that comes with practicing a

6S. Tyler, "Post-Modern Ethnography: From Document of the Occult to Occult Document," in Clifford and Marcus, *Writing Culture*, pp. 130–31; the parenthetical quotation in the next paragraph is from p. 134.

profession inherited from contemporaries of Kipling and Lyautey, there is the authorial self-doubt that comes from practicing it in an academy beset with paradigms, epistemes, language games, *Vorurteile*, epoches, illocutionary acts, S/s, *problématiques*, intentionalities, aporia, and *écriture*— "How to Do Things with Words"; "Must We Mean What We Say?"; "*il n'y a pas de hors-texte*"; "The Prison House of Language." The inadequacy of words to experience, and their tendency to lead off only into other words, has been something both poets and mathematicians long have known; but it is rather a new discovery so far as ethnographers are concerned, and it has put them, or some of them, into something of a disarray, perhaps permanent, probably not.

《》

The disarray may not be permanent, because the anxieties that provoke it may prove masterable with a clearer recognition of their proper origin. The basic problem is neither the moral uncertainty involved in telling stories about how other people live nor the epistemological one involved in casting those stories in scholarly genres—both of which are real enough, are always there, and go with the territory. The problem is that now that such matters are coming to be discussed in the open, rather than covered over with a professional mystique, the burden of authorship seems suddenly heavier. Once ethnographic texts begin to be looked *at* as well as through, once they are seen to be made, and made to persuade, those who make them have rather more to answer for. Such a situation may initially alarm, producing back-to-the-facts table thumping in the establishment and will-to-power gauntlet throwing in its adversaries. But it can, given tenacity enough and courage, be gotten used to.

Whether the period immediately ahead leads to a renewal of the discursive energies of anthropology or to their dissipation, a recovery of authorial nerve or its loss, depends on whether the field (or, more exactly, its would-be practitioners) can adjust itself to a situation in which its goals, its relevance, its motives, and its procedures all are questioned. The "founders of discursivity" reviewed above (and a number of others at least as consequential not reviewed), who brought the field to its present form, themselves had enormous problems of formulation and persuasion to overcome; the suspension of disbelief has never here been particularly willing. But they were spared at least much in the way of assaults upon the justifiability of their enterprise, or upon the sheer possibility of carrying it out. What they were doing may have been odd, but it was admirable, may have been difficult, but it could to some reasonable level be accomplished. To write ethnography now is to write in the realization that such presuppositions are dead, both in author and audience. Neither presumption of innocence nor benefit of doubt is automatically accorded; indeed, save for correlation coefficients and significance tests, they are not accorded at all.

Half-convinced writers trying to half-convince readers of their (the writers') half-convictions would not on the face of it seem an especially favorable situation for the production of works of very much power, ones that could, whatever their failings, do what those of Lévi-Strauss, Evans-Pritchard, Malinowski, and Benedict clearly did: enlarge the sense of how life can go. Yet that is what must happen if the business is to continue; and if either mere digging in ("Don't think about ethnography, just do it") or mere flying off ("Don't do ethnography, just think about it") can be avoided, it should be possible. All that is needed is comparable art.

To say it is art—rather than some lesser achievement

like expertise or some greater like enlightenment—that is most immediately involved in keeping the genre alive and active is also to say the burden of authorship cannot be evaded, however heavy it may have grown; there is no possibility of displacing it onto "method," "language," or (an especially popular maneuver at the moment) "the people themselves" redescribed ("appropriated" is probably the better term) as co-authors. If there is any way to counter the conception of ethnography as an iniquitous act or an unplayable game, it would seem to involve owning up to the fact that, like quantum mechanics or the Italian opera, it is a work of the imagination, less extravagant than the first, less methodical than the second. The responsibility for ethnography, or the credit, can be placed at no other door than that of the romancers who have dreamt it up.

To argue (point out, actually, for, like aerial perspective or the Pythagorean theorem, the thing once seen cannot then be unseen) that the writing of ethnography involves telling stories, making pictures, concocting symbolisms, and deploying tropes is commonly resisted, often fiercely, because of a confusion, endemic in the West since Plato at least, of the imagined with the imaginary, the fictional with the false, making things out with making them up. The strange idea that reality has an idiom in which it prefers to be described, that its very nature demands we talk about it without fuss—a spade is a spade, a rose is a rose—on pain of illusion, trumpery, and self-bewitchment, leads on to the even stranger idea that, if literalism is lost, so is fact.

This can't be right, or else almost all the writings discussed in this book, major and minor alike (as well as virtually all the ethnographies now appearing), would have to be held as lacking reference to anything real. Sheer this-is-ahawk-that-is-a-handsaw writing is actually very rare in anthropology beyond the level of the field report or the topical survey, and it is not upon such journeyman works that the field bases its claim to general attention, but on the glistening towers built by the likes of Lévi-Strauss, Evans-Pritchard, Malinowski, and Benedict. The pretense of looking at the world directly, as though through a one-way screen, seeing others as they really are when only God is looking, is indeed quite widespread. But that is itself a rhetorical strategy, a mode of persuasion; one it may well be difficult wholly to abandon and still be read, or wholly to maintain and still be believed. It is not clear just what "faction," imaginative writing about real people in real places at real times, exactly comes to beyond a clever coinage; but anthropology is going to have to find out if it is to continue as an intellectual force in contemporary culture—if its mule condition (trumpeted scientific mother's brother, disowned literary father) is not to lead to mule sterility.

The "intermediary" nature of at least most ethnographical writing, between author-saturated texts like *David Copperfield* and author-evacuated ones like "On the Electrodynamics of Moving Bodies" (to return to the conceit with which this inquiry began), remains as much the crux, now that anthropologists are caught up in the vast reorganization of political relationships going on in the world and the hardly less vast rethinking of just what it might be that "description" is, as it was when the first had scarcely begun and the second not begun at all. Their task is still to demonstrate, or more exactly to demonstrate again, in different times and with different means, that accounts of how others live that are presented neither as tales about things that did not actually happen, nor as reports of measurable phenomena produced by calculable forces, can carry conviction. Mytho-poetic modes of discourse (*The Divine Comedy, Little Red Riding Hood*) and objectivist ones (*On the Origin of Species, The Farmer's Almanac*) have their own adequacy to their own ends. But, a few oddities aside, ethnography, now as always, neither treats its materials as occasions for revelatory make-believe nor represents them as naturally emergent from an absolutized world.

《》

There are dangers in regarding the anthropological vocation as in important respects a literary one. The enterprise may be seen as turning, like certain varieties of linguistic philosophy, on the meaning of words, its central quarrels all conceptual ones, endlessly dissected, endlessly unresolved—"What (or where) is Culture?" "Can Society be said to cause Behavior?" "Does Kinship exist?" "Do Institutions think?" It may be regarded as so much verbal seduction: rhetorical artifice designed to move intellectual goods in a competitive market. Or, perhaps most popularly, now that the world seems populated with class hypocrisy, false consciousness, and secret agendas, it may be taken to be (rank) ideology in the guise of (dispassionate) science—a mask to be struck through, an imposture to be exposed. And there is, as always when style is attended to and genre underlined, the risk of aestheticism, the possibility that both ethnographers and their audience may come to believe that the value of writing about tattooing or witchcraft exhausts itself in the pleasures of the text. Anthropology as a good read.

But the risks are worth running, and not only because some central issues do in fact revolve about what language games we choose to play, or because neither product enhancement nor tendentious argument is exactly unknown in the increasingly desperate scramble to be noticed, or because writing to please has something to be said for it, at least as against writing to intimidate. The risks are worth running because running them leads to a thoroughgoing revision of our understanding of what it is to open (a bit) the consciousness of one group of people to (something of) the life-form of another, and in that way to (something of) their own. What it is (a task at which no one ever does more than not utterly fail) is to inscribe a present—to convey in words "what it is like" to be somewhere specific in the lifeline of the world: *Here*, as Pascal famously said, rather than *There*; *Now* rather than *Then*.[7] Whatever else ethnography may be— Malinowskian experience seeking, Lévi-Straussian rage for order, Benedictine cultural irony, or Evans-Pritchardish cultural reassurance—it is above all a rendering of the actual, a vitality phrased.

This capacity to persuade readers (most of them academic, virtually all of them at least part-time participants in that peculiar form of existence evasively called "modern") that what they are reading is an authentic account by someone personally acquainted with how life proceeds in some place, at some time, among some group, is the basis upon which anything else ethnography seeks to do—analyze, explain, amuse, disconcert, celebrate, edify, excuse, astonish,

[7]Not only, of course, in words: films and museum displays also play a role, if to date an ancillary one. Nor need the present inscribed be contemporaneous, instantaneous, or exotic; there is ethnography of how things went among disappeared peoples, of the vicissitudes of societies across extended periods of time, and of groups to which the ethnographer belongs, all of which raise special problems (including variant conceptions of what "Being There" involves), but not unsimilar ones. For a discussion of understanding "what it is like" to be someone else, and thus oneself, as a motive for ethnography, see C. Geertz, "The Uses of Diversity," in S. McMurrin, ed., *The Tanner Lectures on Human Values*, vol. 7 (Cambridge, Eng., 1986), pp. 253–75. The "What it is like to be . . ." trope is, of course, taken (and twisted) from Thomas Nagel's seminal, "What Is It Like to Be a Bat?" *Philosophical Review*, 83 (1979): 435–51.

subvert—finally rests.[8] The textual connection of the Being Here and Being There sides of anthropology, the imaginative construction of a common ground between the Written At and the Written About (who are nowadays, as mentioned, not infrequently the same people in a different frame of mind) is the *fons et origo* of whatever power anthropology has to convince anyone of anything—not theory, not method, not even the aura of the professorial chair, consequential as these last may be.

Such a construction of such a ground, now that easy assumptions about the convergence of interests among peoples (sexes, races, classes, cults, . . .) of unequal power have been historically exploded and the very possibility of unconditioned description has come into question, does not look nearly so straightforward an enterprise as it did when hierarchy was in place and language weightless. The moral asymmetries across which ethnography works and the discoursive complexity within which it works make any attempt to portray it as anything more than the representation of one sort of life in the categories of another impossible to defend. That may be enough. I, myself, think that it is. But it spells the end of certain pretensions.

There are a number of these pretensions, but they all tend to come down in one way or another to an attempt to get round the un-get-roundable fact that all ethnographical

[8]Again, it must be explicitly noted that ethnography may be second order (as it is for the most part with Lévi-Strauss and Benedict) and the "Being There" effect thus derivative. Much of the "ethnographized" history that has recently become popular—Emmanuel Le Roi Ladurie, *Montaillou* (London, 1978; first published 1975) and *Carnival in Romans* (New York, 1980; first published 1976); Robert Darnton, *The Great Cat Massacre* (New York, 1986); Rhys Isaac, *The Transformation of Virginia, 1740–1790* (Chapel Hill, N.C., 1982); Natalie Zemon Davis, *The Return of Martin Guerre* (Cambridge, Mass., 1983)—importantly rests on such an effect, produced not, of course, by the authors' representing themselves as having literally "been there," but by their basing their analyses on the experiential disclosures of people who were.

descriptions are homemade, that they are the describer's descriptions, not those of the described.

There is ethnographic ventriloquism: the claim to speak not just *about* another form of life but to speak from within it; to represent a depiction of how things look from "an Ethiopian (woman poet's) point of view" as itself an Ethiopian (woman poet's) depiction of how they look from such a view. There is text positivism: the notion that, if only Emawayish can be got to dictate or write down her poems as carefully as possible and they are translated as faithfully as possible, then the ethnographer's role dissolves into that of an honest broker passing on the substance of things with only the most trivial of transaction costs. There is dispersed authorship: the hope that ethnographic discourse can somehow be made "heteroglossial," so that Emawayish can speak within it alongside the anthropologist in some direct, equal, and independent way; a There presence in a Here text. There is confessionalism: the taking of the ethnographer's experience rather than its object as the primary subject matter for analytical attention, portraying Emawayish in terms of the effect she has on those who encounter her; a There shadow of a Here reality. And there is, most popularly of all, the simple assumption that although Emawayish and her poems are, of course, inevitably seen through an author-darkened glass, the darkening can be minimized by authorial self-inspection for "bias" or "subjectivity," and she and they can then be seen face to face.

All this is not to say that descriptions of how things look to one's subjects, efforts to get texts exact and translations veridical, concern with allowing to the people one writes about an imaginative existence in one's text corresponding to their actual one in their society, explicit reflection upon what field work does or doesn't do to the field worker, and rigorous examination of one's assumptions are not supremely worth doing for anyone who aspires to tell someone leading a French sort of life what leading an Ethiopian one is like. It is to say that doing so does not relieve one of the burden of authorship; it deepens it. Getting Emawayish's views right, rendering her poems accessible, making her reality perceptible, and clarifying the cultural framework within which she exists, means getting them sufficiently onto the page that someone can obtain some comprehension of what they might be. This is not only a difficult business, it is one not without consequence for "native," "author," and "reader" (and, indeed, for that eternal victim of other people's activities, "innocent bystander") alike.

《 》

Like any cultural institution, anthropology—which is a rather minor one compared with law, physics, music, or cost accounting—is of a place and in a time, perpetually perishing, not so certainly perpetually renewing. The energies that created it, first in the nineteenth century (when it tended to be a sweeping, up-from-the-ape, study-of-mankind sort of business), and then in the earlier part of this century (when it came to focus on particular peoples as crystal wholes, isolate and entire), were certainly connected, if rather more complexly than commonly represented, both with the imperial expansion of the West and with the rise there of a salvational belief in the powers of science.[9] Since the Second World War, the dissolution of colonialism and the appearance of a more realistic view of science have rather

[9] For the earlier period, a detailed and balanced treatment can now be found in G. W. Stocking, Jr., *Victorian Anthropology* (New York, 1987). A comparable integral study for this century, when the relationships grew even more intricate, is not yet available.

dissipated these energies. Neither the role of intercultural middleman, shuttling back and forth between the Euro-American centers of world power and various exotic elsewheres so as to mediate between the prejudices of the one and the parochialisms of the other, nor that of transcultural theoretician, bringing odd beliefs and unusual social structures under general laws, is anywhere nearly so available to anthropologists as they once were. And thus the question arises: What *is* available? What is, now that the proconsuls are gone and sociomechanics implausible, the next necessary thing?

There is, of course, no single answer to this question, nor can answers be given before the fact, before anthropological authors actually author them. *Ex ante* prescriptive criticism—this is what you must do, that is what you must not—is as absurd in anthropology as it is in any other intellectual enterprise not dogmatically based. Like poems and hypotheses, ethnographies can only be judged *ex post*, after someone has brought them into being. But, for all that, it seems likely that whatever use ethnographic texts will have in the future, if in fact they actually have any, it will involve enabling conversation across societal lines—of ethnicity, religion, class, gender, language, race—that have grown progressively more nuanced, more immediate, and more irregular. The next necessary thing (so at least it seems to me) is neither the construction of a universal Esperanto-like culture, the culture of airports and motor hotels, nor the invention of some vast technology of human management. It is to enlarge the possibility of intelligible discourse between people quite different from one another in interest, outlook, wealth, and power, and yet contained in a world where, tumbled as they are into endless connection, it is increasingly difficult to get out of each other's way.

This world, one of a gradual spectrum of mixed-up differences, is the one in which any would-be founders of discursivity must now, and quite probably for some time to come, operate. Lévi-Strauss, Evans-Pritchard, Malinowski, and Benedict operated in a world of a more discontinuous assemblage of more separated differences (the Bororo, the Zande, the Trobrianders, the Zuni), and the great polyhistors (Tylor, Morgan, Frazer, etc.) they displaced operated in one of an immense dichotomy of the improving civilized and the improvable savage. The There's and the Here's, much less insulate, much less well-defined, much less spectacularly contrastive (but no less deeply so) have again changed their nature. If the enterprise—creating works that relate the one to the other in some intelligible fashion—has remained recognizably continuous, the way of accomplishing it, indeed what accomplishing it amounts to, must clearly alter. Ethnographers have now to do with realities with which neither encyclopedism nor monographism, world surveys nor tribal studies, can practically cope. Something new having emerged both in "the field" and in "the academy," something new must appear on the page.

Some signs that this fact is at least vaguely appreciated, if not fully understood, can be found in all sorts of places in contemporary anthropology, and efforts are being made, some of them impressive, more of them less so, to come to terms with it. The present state of play in the field is at once disordered and inventive, haphazard and various.[10] But it has been that before and found a direction. What it hasn't been, and, propelled by the moral and intellectual self-confidence of Western Civilization, hasn't so much had to

[10]More specific assessments would be invidious here, and premature. For my general view of the field at the moment, see "Waddling In," *Times Literary Supplement*, June 7, 1985 (no. 4,288), pp. 623–24.

148

be, is aware of the sources of its power. If it is now to prosper, with that confidence shaken, it must become aware. Attention to how it gets its effects and what those are, to anthropology on the page, is no longer a side issue, dwarfed by problems of method and issues of theory. It, and Emawayish's question, is rather close to the heart of the matter.

INDEX

INDEX

INDEX